EAVESDROPPING

EAVESDROPPING

A Life by Ear

Stephen Kuusisto

W. W. NORTON & COMPANY

NEW YORK • LONDON

For information about permission to reproduce selections from this book, write to
Permissions, W. W. Norton & Company, Inc., 500 Fifth Avenue, New York, NY 10110

Manufacturing by The Courier Companies, Inc.
Book design by Dana Sloan
Production manager: Amanda Morrison

Library of Congress Cataloging-in-Publication Data

Kuusisto, Stephen.
Eavesdropping : a life by ear / Stephen Kuusisto. — 1st ed.
p. cm.
ISBN-13: 978-0-393-34958-0

1. Kuusisto, Stephen. 2. Poets, American—20th century—Biography.
3. Blind—United States—Biography. I. Title.
PS3561.U85Z46 2006
811'.6—dc22

2006009920

W. W. Norton & Company, Inc., 500 Fifth Avenue, New York, N.Y. 10110
www.wwnorton.com

W. W. Norton & Company Ltd., Castle House, 75/76 Wells Street, London W1T 3QT

1 2 3 4 5 6 7 8 9 0

For Connie

In order to create there must be a dynamic force,
and what force is more potent than love?

—IGOR STRAVINSKY

CONTENTS

TWO: *"Walking by Ear"*

Preface

——◆——

A few years ago I wrote a memoir entitled *Planet of the Blind*. In that book I described growing up with a visual impairment in the late fifties and sixties. I was lonely as a child and lived in rural New Hampshire, Finland, and western New York, locales that compounded the isolation of blindness. Like many children with disabilities, I was eager to be a part of the world around me and capable of denial if denying my blindness allowed me to join in the activities of "normal" children. I simply lowered my head and ran forward into the patterns of light and shade that make up my kind of vision loss. This was not an ideal way to live but at least I was unsupervised and on the street in an era when that posture wasn't customary for disabled children.

Happily I no longer crave recognition as a sighted person. At fifty I've learned how to be as much of myself as possible. Like many others before me, I learned some of this acceptance from an exceptional dog. In 1994, when I was thirty-nine, I went to Guiding Eyes for the Blind, one of America's premier guide-dog training schools, and there I was paired with my first guide dog, Corky, a yellow Labrador retriever. Corky knew instinctively how to live in the world, and walking beside her I experienced a new delight in traveling. Together we visited hundreds of cities: "invisible cities," as Italo Calvino would say. Corky watched the traffic in Milan, San Francisco, New Orleans, or Venice, and I did all the listening.

It was during a visit to Boston with Corky that the scheme for this book first occurred to me. I had just delivered a talk to blind people at the Carroll Center—a nonprofit agency which assists people with visual impairments. I had been talking about the pleasures and advantages of navigating with a guide dog and we had arrived at the question-and-answer period. There were about a dozen folks in the audience, all of them newly blind, and most of the questions were about how to apply for a guide dog or how walking with a dog differs from traveling with a white cane. Suddenly a woman called out from the back of the room. Her voice was fierce. "Why travel anywhere if you can't see?" she asked. Her words seemed to linger in the air. I tried to ask her questions to defuse the awkwardness of the moment. This woman was in her mid-fifties; she'd gone blind from diabetes; her husband had recently passed away—her question was complex and it had a good deal to do with faith. What would the future hold? What is the use of going forward? Without eyesight aren't we "selfless" in the worst sense? How can one live in a world without independence or the daily therapy of sight-seeing?

My answer was too quick. I said that one can hear baroque music in Venice or dine on softshell crabs in Baltimore. I think I also said something about the good endorphins of a brisk morning's walk. But I knew as we wrapped things up that I hadn't answered her question.

Veteran blind people know that it's possible to sight-see by ear, for we do it all the time. Alone in unfamiliar hotel lobbies, we survey our surroundings and hear in the ambient curves of architecture a hundred oddities. We hear the movements of strangers; hear their laughter; hear pennies dropped in the Hilton's fountain; the bristles of a shoeshine brush; the wings of a pigeon that has made its way indoors. The blind hear all this while they're locating the chiming bells of the elevators.

Blindness often leads to compensatory listening (if one has the fortune of a hearing life). In *Planet of the Blind* I describe how I listened to teachers when I was a small boy and developed an auditory version of what was happening around me. Unable to see the chalkboard or read a standard book, I learned by necessity how to hear both for content and splendor.

I used the term "compensatory listening" just now but I could substitute "creative listening." Blind people are not casual eavesdroppers. We have method. As things happen around us we reinvent what we hear like courtroom artists who sketch as fast as they can. We are also cartoonists of a sort: our sketches are both clear and improbable. I am essentially an inept landscape painter. I draw unlikely trees and mechanical people in the manner of Max Ernst. In reality I cannot see the world by ear, I can only reinvent it for my own purposes. But admitting this may make me lucky. I am free to daydream for survival or amusement. Even when I listen to Manhattan traffic I'm drawing my own pictures of New York—the streets are crowded with Russian ghosts and wheels that have broken loose from their carriages.

After my trip to Boston I wondered what a book about living or traveling by ear might be like. It would, I realized, probably develop without a dramatic scenario. Knowing and savoring the world by ear is really an impressionistic subject. Was it possible to write a memoir about what my ears know? Such a book would have to contain what the poet Wallace Stevens called "the

pleasures of merely circulating." It would have to be a collection
of auditory postcards or "tone poems." This is how I navigate the
world. I enter unfamiliar environments and I listen with everything I have, finding inchoate music in what happens around me.
As I considered this I remembered that the Finnish composer
Sibelius wrote tone poems for the orchestra. He envisioned them
as musical paintings, "impressionistic" paintings that would
remind his countrymen how mysterious and beautiful the world
really was.

Even though a lyric style has its virtues, there are some
things the reader of this book might want to know, particularly
if he or she hasn't read *Planet of the Blind*. The most important
matter may have to do with how blind people "see." My own
version of blindness is known as retinopathy of prematurity.
Children who are born prematurely can, in some instances, have
damaged retinas. Blind people who have this condition often see
the world in fragments. One sees like a myopic, darting min-
now. This kind of seeing is both beautiful and worrisome. Many
additional forms of blindness also produce these sorts of effects.
People with macular degeneration see shifting islands of darkness and jumping apertures of sight. Diabetic retinopathy leaves
one in a field of muddy light. Cataracts are like having Vaseline
in your eyes. In any event the majority of blind people see small
glimpses of the world, though these views are inaccurate. That
the blind see anything at all is, however, often surprising to
many people.

It is also helpful to know that I was ashamed of my disability throughout my childhood and this sadness was compounded
by my mother's militant refusal to use the words "blind" or
"blindness." In the early sixties disabled children did not attend
public schools and my mother insisted that I should receive a
public education. Accordingly I became a soldier of denial and

lived in nervous self-absorption. The Americans with Disabilities Act was thirty years away in an unimaginable future. My job was to live in the open without words for my circumstances. This is not an uncommon tale, as many people with disabilities will tell you.

And so by necessity I learned how to savor the world by ear. The first section of this book concerns childhood. I realize now that I had the good fortune to live my early years in provincial places. My father was a professor at the University of New Hampshire and we lived in the woods. We also lived in Helsinki, Finland, when that rare and beautiful city was largely an unknown destination for tourists. I heard reindeer bells and ancient folk songs long before I heard a transistor radio.

Part two of this memoir is concerned with adult travel, much of it in the company of my first guide dog, Corky. When Corky retired and became my family's house pet she was succeeded by another yellow Labrador named Vidal. Vidal turns up in several of the chapters or auditory postcards in section two.

Finally, since this book is entirely concerned with the art of listening, there are a few additional biographical details about the narrator that might be helpful to know. I now live in Columbus, Ohio, where I teach in the English department at the Ohio State University. I am married to Connie Rudloff, who was for over twenty years both an administrator and trainer of guide dogs at Guiding Eyes for the Blind. We got married in Jamaica in Bob Marley's parish in 1998. Connie appears in the Venice section of this book. She's a tireless advocate for people with disabilities and she is the love of my life. She continues to help me travel by ear. She recently agreed to be my sighted running companion in a marathon.

As a final point (and still in the sphere of biography), I like this remark by Igor Stravinsky. He once said, "To listen is an effort, and just to hear is no merit. A duck hears also." The pages that follow are about a life of effort. I have been lucky sometimes to find places where I could work by ear and pause for whole moments, receiving treasures of sound and sense.

Stephen Kuusisto
Rattlesnake Island
Alton, New Hampshire
July 2005

One

"SWEET LONGINGS"

What if you forgot how to bring inside
the music that used to begin
in your gradual wakings, and in the space
before sleep, when rain began softly,
and all your sweet longings loosened.

—Susan Ludvigson, "What If"

1. Harbor Songs

My first memory of hearing comes from the Baltic. I remember my father holding my hand as we walked to the end of a jetty in Helsinki, Finland. Although it was late in March, Finland was still bitterly cold and the harbor was dotted with ice.

My form of blindness allowed me to see colors and torn geometries. Shards of ice drifted past us and my father told me they looked like continents. "There's Australia," he said. "There's Hawaii." But when I looked out I saw no distinction between sky and ice. I saw only endless plains of gray Baltic light. This didn't bother me. It was the world I knew. It was a world of shadowy loves. If a person appeared before me he or she resembled nothing more than the black trunk of a tree.

We turned back and walked toward shore. A troupe of women emerged from the mist. They were indistinct, liquid, black and green. These were the old women from the neighborhood unfurling their carpets on the shore of the frozen sea.

Lordy! Then they sang!

The tree women sang and beat their carpets in the Baltic wind.

My father told me to listen.

"These are the old songs," he said.

The women croaked, chanted, breathed, and wept.

The women were forest people. They had survived starvation, civil war, and then another war, the "Winter War" with the Russians.

Their carpets swayed on wooden racks that stood along the shore. They sang and beat dust from the rugs with sticks.

They sang over and over a song of night. The song unwound from a spool. I remember its terrible darkness. They were together singing a song that rose from a place deeper than dreams. Even a boy knows what this is.

From 1958 to 1960 my parents and I lived in the south harbor of Helsinki, just a short walk from the open-air market where fish peddlers and butchers had their stalls. We walked across the cobbled square and I'd tilt my head in the gray light and listen to the gulls and ravens. The gulls sounded like mewing cats and the ravens sounded like hinges in need of oil. I walked about listening to the polyphony of hungry birds.

The Russian Orthodox Church had mysterious chimes.

And winter wouldn't give up. We traveled into the country and I heard the reindeer bells. At an old farm I heard the runners of a sleigh crossing ice. What else?

The woman who sold flowers outside the railway station sang just for me. And her little daughter played a wooden recorder . . .

Wind poured into the city through the masts of sailboats.

There was an old man who sold potatoes from a dory in the harbor. His voice was like sand. He talked to me every day.

Potatoes from the earth, potatoes from the cellar! You can still taste the summer! You can still taste the summer!

Later I would think of his voice when reading of trolls under bridges.

What else?

Sound of knife blades in the tinsmith's stall . . .

The rumble of streetcars . . .

The clacking of a loom . . . My mother weaving a rug . . .

The sound of my father's typing late in the night . . .

Sound of a wooden top that whistled like a teakettle . . . my first toy . . .

A winter tree tapping at the window . . .

My father was a visiting professor at the University of Helsinki and he had time to walk with me and introduce me to the chance music of the city.

One day he took me to the house of a glassblower. This was my first experience of synesthesia: the strange suffusion of one sense with another . . . The glassblower took his long-stemmed pipe out of the flames. I could barely make out the red halo of the fire. The glassblower explained how he pushed his breath into the molten glass and then I heard him inhale. As he leaned into his art there was a spirited cry from a cuckoo clock on the far wall. Delicacy and irreverence have been forever linked in my mind from that very moment.

On the way home we rode the tram and I listened to the wintry talk of the passengers. I loved the sound of Finnish, especially the oddly whispered Finnish of strangers sitting side by side on the tram. The Finns inhale as they speak, a lovely sotto voce confirmation that two minds are in solemn agreement. One could hear whispers and inhalations as twilight covered the city. I talked to the empty seat beside me and spoke Finnish to an imaginary friend whom I named Matti. I held my breath and listened to the rocking of the tram. I exhaled and spoke in a flurry to my little doppelgänger. My father was lost in his newspaper. I was lost on the heart's road of whispered confidences.

The entire world was green or white. Blindness for me was

veil after veil of forest colors. But what a thrill it was to be a sightless child in a city of sounds.

Our apartment was in the south harbor. My mother wove a carpet and listened to the radio. She said that the Russian navy was coming, that it had just been announced. And then we heard the booming of the guns from beyond the archipelago of islands in the Baltic. The Soviet navy was conducting war games and we stood on our balcony and listened to the guns of the destroyers. A neighbor woman told us this was the sound that made her hair turn white. I worried for days that we would all have white hair. I asked my parents all kinds of questions about growing old. Why did the Russians want to make people old? I put such great faith in sound: sound was this tree and that grass; this man; this dimension of light and shade. Meanwhile the evening wind arrived and the Russian navy went away.

April turned to May and the park spun itself into green smoke; leaves filled the trees again; and an old man played his accordion in a grove of birches. A little girl whose name I can no longer recall taught me to waltz. I'm sure that her parents must have told her I was blind. She must have been around eight years old. She swayed me back and forth in the light of the birches. The old man played slowly and I felt something of the Zen-body: wherever I was I was there. By the age of four I'd found the intricacies of listening were inexhaustible.

In 1960 we flew home to the United States. I loved the groan and rumble of the plane's propellers. What a fabulous sound they made! I rested my head against the cabin wall and felt the vibration rattle through my bones. I hummed and let the engines push my own little song. I imitated the Kalevala cadences and sorrows of the Finnish carpet ladies and groaned in unison with the straining metal of the airplane.

2. Horse

———◆———

Maybe it was a Saturday. I remember that my parents were still sleeping. I had a plan and dressed quietly. When I was certain that no one was awake I slipped from the house. I loved to walk in the woods and follow the beams of light or depths of shade that fell between trees. I remember that on this particular day I got lost while chasing light and found myself standing in front of the university's horse barn. I knew that somewhere in the cool space before me a horse was breathing. I stood in the door and listened to him breathe. He sounded like water going down a drain. Then I took one step forward into a pyramid of fragrances.

What a thing! To be a young boy smelling hay and leather and turds!

From his place in the dark the horse gurgled like water in the back of a boat.

Mice scurried like beaded curtains disturbed by a hand.

I stood in that magical nowhere and listened to a full range of barn sounds.

I was a blind child approaching a horse!

Behind me a cat mewed.

Who would guess that horses sometimes hold their breath?

The horse was eyeing me from his corner.

Then two cats were talking.

Wind pushed forcefully at the high roof.

Somewhere up high a timber groaned.

My horse was still holding his breath.

When would he breathe again?

Come on boy!

Breathe for me!

Where are you?

I heard him rub his flank against a wall.

Then I heard him breathe again with a great deflation!

He sounded like a fat balloon venting in swift circles.

And then I imitated him with my arm pressed to my mouth.

I made great, flatulent noises by pressing my lips to my forearm.

How do you like that, horse?

He snorted.

I noticed the ringing of silence. An insect traveled between our bursts of forced air.

Sunlight warmed my face. I was standing in a wide sunbeam.

I was in the luminous whereabouts of horse! I was a very small boy and I had wandered about a mile from home. Although I could see colors and shapes in sunlight, in the barn I was completely blind.

But I had made up my mind to touch a horse.

Judging by his breathing, his slow release of air, that sound of a concertina, judging by this I was nearly beside him. And so I reached out and there was the great wet fruit of his nose, the velvet bone of his enormous face. And we stood there together for a little while, all alive and all alone.

At night when I couldn't sleep I thought of this horse. I

thought of his glory—his fat sound. I thought of how he pinched the air around him with his breathing. The house and the trees swayed in the night wind. The horse was dry wood talking. He was all nerves and nostrils. He tightened and then unwound like a clock. He groaned like the Finnish women who stood beside the ocean waving their sticks. Strophe and antistrophe. Step. Rhythm. Pulse beat. I'd crossed a threshold, hearing and walking the uncertain space that opened before me . . .

3. Birds

———◆———

By seven I was old enough to get the picture. Disability left me with time on my hands. It would be another thirty years before physical education for disabled kids would become widespread. Sometimes from the edge of the field I listened to the neighbor's children playing softball, but without description this was a marginal entertainment.

I walked in the woods, trying to locate the flower known as the lady's slipper—a violet-going-to-rose-colored orchid. Seeing only colors, I spent hours searching for this prize.

There were paths beside a creek descending into stands of bullrushes.

A catbird appeared in the trees above me and I talked back to him.

I knew the birds from a radio program. I'd wake early on Sundays and listen to a solemn old man guiding listeners through the calls of New Hampshire's birds. The purple finch sounded more contented than any creature I knew of. He sounded like the world's fastest wind chimes. The old man and the purple finch gave me my first lesson in timbre. "Sounds," he said, "even bird sounds, have character. A nagging blue jay makes flat notes. Birds in love are very round." The finch's notes were round and quick as pins dropping on a glass table. Alone in the woods, I could spend a whole hour listening to a single bird. I had a bed of moss where I'd lie for the concert. The moss smelled like bread. My hands were sticky with pine pitch. I lay there a long time.

My early childhood occurred in the last moments of unmediated listening. The transistor radio was too new for wide distribution. The television was an evening device and largely controlled by adults. One simply walked in the ambient and stratified air of the birds.

Blackbirds from a willow rattled like paper fans.

Then there was the whippoorwill who simply sounded like himself.

Behind him was the pine warbler with his stretched song . . .

I knew that when the birds were alone they acted differently than in flocks. I listened for solo birds: the eastern phoebe, the hermit thrush, the vesper sparrow, the swamp sparrow . . .

The vesper sparrow started by singing *sweet, sweet, sweet* . . .

The grosbeak was a wire unwinding.

I heard the downy woodpecker. The northern flicker . . .

I was supremely theirs. The marsh wren, the veery, Swainson's thrush . . .

They moved from branch to branch.

The goldfinch. Eastern meadowlark . . .

I learned to follow the movements and voice of a single thrush.

The thrush produced point notes like strings played pizzicato on a violin. First he was in the audible field of my left ear. And I held still. There was the whine of a mosquito, the slow vibrato of a bee. Red squirrels chattered and dodged in the underbrush. Then the thrush poured out dozens of notes and I could sense exactly where he was. He was high in a white pine, a tree that had numerous long-dead branches protruding from its trunk. I thought of the tree as having witch's arms. He was up there. He was still in the circle of my left ear. He was very alive. He was throwing darts of sound and his tempo was fast as a bird's heart would allow. I thought of a dying thrush that I had held in my hand, its heart like the clatter of twigs caught in bicycle spokes.

Then he stopped singing for maybe thirty seconds. And there he was again, singing into my right ear. It was definitely him, the voice unmistakable. My secret purple thrush, my fist-sized harpsichordist.

Alone at night in my room, I pushed an olivewood camel, a trinket from a Middle Eastern tourist shop, across a window. The glass squeaked at the touch of the camel's feet. I pushed these sounds before me like flags.

I lay awake long into the night.

I said the Lord's Prayer though my voice was scarcely audible. The room was wonderfully cold. A snowy owl talked in his owl code—three calls—then silence for the same duration—then three more calls. He was a singer out of nowhere.

The birds offered me their audible contours and perspectives. By day the blackbird cried from the tunnel of his fever. The nuthatch sang like rain falling into a tin dish. These birds became my foreground. And a herring gull called because he was following the Oyster River and saw something glitter in the leaves.

One morning I found the wild orchid. I was just following the high song of a pheasant through the leaves, crawling on my hands and knees. The lady's slipper was a dainty curl of petals and I heard the scrabbling feet of the pheasants in the leaves and I lay down to let the mauves and violets into my eyes. And the pheasants circled like all walking birds, dry-dancing around me in formation.

4. Ice

———◆———

Sometimes ice would form between the trees behind my house. I walked among the pines because I was lucky and small and the ice would hold me. But as I moved the ice moved. I heard how it shifted in more than one way. I took a step and a bubble of air jumped like a mouse under my feet and the rolling, trapped air sounded like a very tiny spoon striking a glass. I took another innocent step. Again the spoon. Then the air rolled into the roots of a tree where it made no more noise. I could picture that bubble of air down in the tangle of roots. And then I lay on the ice and put my ear to the surface. I heard the ice shift and groan like a plank. And then I rolled across the open ice and listened to the creaking and laughing of ice and frozen wood. I was thrilled to discover I could influence the percussive speech of the frozen world.

I rolled too fast then. Ice broke beneath me. There was no water underneath, only air. The ice came in around me like silver coins. I rolled and felt shards of ice around my cheekbones and in my hair. Ice got up under my jacket and clicked like twigs caught in a wheel. What good music this was! It was instantaneous and my little boy's mind could make sounds happen and the world smelled of fresh snow.

There was a wire fence in the woods and I found that I could play it like a harp. The fence was rusted and frozen and it sagged among rocks. If you plucked it with a finger it sounded like a dark piano string.

And birch trees swayed, their skins of ice making a bright, sympathetic sunlit music. I shook the birches one by one and was rewarded with the sound of ice skittering down from the high branches. I loved that confusion of ice with its thousand tiny blades all cutting at the light.

In the house, down in the basement, my mother collected large metal drums. She was quietly building a bomb shelter in a pitch-black corner. She stacked metal drums that were intended to hold drinking water but she never filled them. I found that I could play them as instruments, tapping them with my fingers, or opening the cans I put marbles inside so I could hear them roll. Over forty years later, sitting with my wife in Carnegie Hall, I heard an intricate postmodern concerto by Mstislav Rostropovich and I knew at once he too had been a lonely child. One simply pushes his or her homemade music and gets through the dark that way. And some children are noticed by their parents and perhaps they're lucky and their parents buy them instruments. At La Scala, the opera house in Milan, one can see Giuseppe Verdi's boyhood piano. Pencil marks have been drawn across the keys—the notes scrawled by Verdi's father so his little boy could find his way through the forest of sound.

And then there are those children who simply play with ice.

5. Victrola

In the summer of 1962 I was sent to live with my grandmother in the old resort town of Laconia, New Hampshire. At her home two things became immediately apparent. Just like my mother, my grandmother liked to sleep through the afternoon. But my grandmother seemed to have no friends. She lived solely in the world of her Victorian house.

It was August and wet and rain struck at the tall windows until they sounded like snare drums. I thought of British soldiers striding through Concord. I thought of the troops in Washington's army marching in the rain. And so I decided to be a soldier and walk outside. It was early afternoon and my grandmother was sound asleep.

I followed a crooked path down to the old garage.

Rain pounded on abandoned steel drums in the uncut grass. There was a way to crawl under the garage at the rear of the building. I went under it and slithered on my stomach and toads made way for me in the dead leaves. Streams poured in runnels alongside the garage. I fell asleep in my burrow.

It rained for ten consecutive days, and over the long hours, hours when I was far too much on my own, I found my way to the top of my grandmother's decaying house. At the top of a dusty staircase I discovered a heavy door. Behind it I could hear the fluttering of wings. There were birds or bats in there. I knew my grandmother most likely had a broken window.

The attic was enormous and there were pigeons and squirrels and hornets making separate declarations. The hornets had their own corner beside a window and I knew it would be simple enough to leave them alone. But I did sit down and listen to them for a time. They flew in small orbits around the room. I remember my surprise when I found that they could fly past my head without making a sound. I simply heard a rent in the still air as the hornet flew by in a straight line.

Other hornets hit the window and made a noise like thrown buttons.

I found another door and stepped into a room that was full of wingbeats. Pigeons rose wildly to the ceiling beams when I pushed the door. I pressed my way in and listened as one by one the birds found their mysterious way out. There were quick rustlings as they vanished.

It was in the next room that I found my first Victrola.

The old machine stood on a table, its horn imperial.

With my minimal sight I could see the inflorescence of spiderwebs and soot.

I stood still for a minute, and when I was satisfied that the Victrola wasn't dangerous I touched it.

At once the platter turned and there was a groan!

The long needle was still perched in the groove of a disk.

I turned the record with my finger and produced a pitiless, unformed sound, a noise like a wrought-iron hinge. When I turned the record again I heard the raging wind from some unidentifiable continent.

I pictured the neck of the horn: a black maw, holding men, faces, eyes, and opened hands.

Sound, like love, can be sudden and threatening.

In that attic, turning the record, I felt the pulse of my discovery. I stayed until sunset.

The next day I climbed the forgotten stairs again and found that by turning the handle I could set the record spinning freely.

The recording was Caruso's "Vesti la giubba."

Years later I would find out that this was the best-selling recording of the twentieth century until Elvis Presley surpassed it with "All Shook Up."

In the teens and early twenties people bought Caruso's recordings when they bought their record machines. They were buying tragedy by the truckload.

I listened to Canio, the clown and murderer . . . the hollow needle . . . a noise of pitching metal and wax . . . It sounded as if a vital man was singing through a steam pipe from a room in a cellar.

Then the frightful laughter . . . I ran each time I heard it . . . the cachinnation of a madman suddenly rose from the enormous bell of the trumpet . . .

I had to return to the attic a dozen times that summer before I could finally hear the aria in full.

The Victrola sang from its great, crackling heart.

And my own heart raced.

6. House Music

———◆———

My grandmother seemed to live only to smoke cigarettes. She smoked languidly, lighting Kents with a Zippo. The lighter clicked shut like a lock.

I heard the far sound of squeaking pulleys. A woman was hanging laundry in the sun.

Someone was hammering at an even greater distance. But whoever held the hammer was uncertain.

A tamarack tree had grown unkempt and leaned into the porch. Its needles stirred against the handrail.

My grandmother smoked with perfect delicacy. The Zippo came out again.

She was a woman of silences. I never saw her in the company of others.

A chickadee called from his upside-down perch. Even as a little boy I thought of the chickadee as a bird of superficial happiness. He cried *fee-bee-bee* as if the circus was coming. I wanted to tell him it was only a mournful day in summer at my grandmother's enormous and vaguely frightening house.

"Listen," my grandmother said without warning. "Can you

hear that?" She didn't say what the "that" might be. I listened though.

From far down the street came a sputtering sound. A sound like a huge motorized teakettle. It was definitely a machine noise. It seemed far away and it was moving slowly.

"That's a Model A Ford," my grandmother said. "An old-fashioned car," she added. "That car must be forty years old."

It drove past us with its strategic and showy motor.

"Do you really know the sound of each car?" I asked.

"Oh yes," she said, "I know the sound of every car ever made."

She sounded mildly surprised that I hadn't known this about her.

"Your grandfather built cars fifty years ago. I've always been interested in cars ever since."

"Hear that?" she said.

I heard the approach of an engine.

"That's a Studebaker!" she said.

"How do you know?" I was surprised to hear myself talking.

"A Studebaker is noisy, like a little locomotive," she said, then added, "It's not a very good car."

I had a new appreciation for my silent and remote grand-mother. She became for me, a blind kid alone in summer—she became my first guru of listening.

"Hear that?" she said. "That's a cowbird. It's the only bird that lays its eggs in another bird's nest. Then it flies away and leaves the owner of the nest to raise its young. It's my favorite bird."

Because we were talking and listening together, she decided to take me to an anteroom just off the front parlor. There was a tall wooden radio that stood alone in a corner.

"Can you see this?" she said. "Here, put your nose on it."

The radio had a green glass eye that glowed when the machine was turned on. With my nose directly on the glass eye I could feel the electricity humming through the huge box.

A burst of static suddenly popped from the speaker and I jumped.

"It's just warming up," my grandmother said. She grabbed my hand and pressed it against a knob.

"This is the knob for changing the stations."

Then she grabbed my other hand.

"This is the knob for the volume. Don't ever turn the volume up. You can listen but I don't want to hear this from my room."

Her room was half a dozen rooms away. I wondered what she could hear. If she could hear the radio from across that distance, how could she sleep so soundly?

She let go of my hands and I sat on the floor.

She tuned a station.

A growl came out.

"That's Arthur Godfrey," she said with a slight rising note of admiration.

Arthur Godfrey mumbled from inside the box of glass tubes and wires. He sounded exhausted. Then he laughed. His laughter also sounded exhausted.

I pressed my nose against the radio's cloth-draped speaker and felt the vibrating laughter on my face. And I smelled dust and the odor of electrical wiring.

"Remember, don't turn it up." My grandmother lingered for a moment, observing me. Then she walked away.

Living in my grandmother's house was so utterly isolating that I started to have a premature sense that I was like a long-distance swimmer. I knew I was swimming through the solo

hours. Looking back, I see how stoic I was. Remembering soli-
tude is to remember how I pressed my face to the cool trunk of
an ironwood tree and closed my eyes and listened to a single
cricket.

My New Hampshire grandfather died the year I was born
but his presence still remained in the house. Those were his
Caruso records in the attic. He had been a manufacturer of early
automobiles and motorcycles. During the First World War he
supplied munitions for the U.S. government. There were still
cases of blasting caps in the cellar alongside the dusty mason jars
and the rotten snowshoes. No one seemed to care that explosives
were slowly becoming unstable down in the basement. I played
in the cellar and used the empty dynamite cartons as fortresses
for my toy soldiers.

One day after spending hours in the basement I climbed the
stairs to the kitchen in search of my grandmother. I'd found a
surplus gas mask and I had no idea what it was.

I looked first in her bedroom, which was just down a corridor from the old servants' kitchen. She wasn't there. I walked
into the front foyer past the grandfather clock and into the living room. No one. I looked in my grandfather's former study. I
climbed the wide stairs to the second floor and nosed along a
corridor.

It came over me that I was alone in the house and there
wasn't a sound from anywhere. There wasn't any traffic noise
outside. No one was mowing a lawn in the neighborhood.

I pressed my face to an oval of leaded glass beside the front
door. I liked the play of speckled light on my eye. I heard suddenly a low muttering that seemed to come from the heart of the
tiny window. *Go away*, said the window. Who was watching
me? Whose voice came from that circle of glass?

My grandmother walked in the back door about an hour

later. She'd been uncharacteristically active, cutting and arranging flowers. I decided not to tell her about the voice.

A night of thunder followed that very same evening. While my grandmother watched *The Lawrence Welk Show* I excused myself and headed for the attic. I'd learned to love lightning storms and I knew the attic was the best place in the world to hear them.

Maybe it was my blindness that allowed me to wander the old attic in a storm without any anxiety. Maybe it had to do with having conquered my fear of the Victrola. Whatever it was, the attic was my favorite place.

The oak beams of the mansard roof were squeaking in the wind. I wound up the Victrola and let Caruso out of his box. I lay on the dusty floor as the lightning zeroed in. I was creating a provincial world from the sounds that were available to me. Thunder rattled the loose glass in a window.

One hot Sunday afternoon I was so lonely I decided to turn on the old radio in the parlor. It stood at least a foot taller than I did. Static snapped from the speaker. I waited for the green eye to glow. I sat while the tubes heated and the wiring hummed. At last I turned the dial and tuned in a station. Glenn Miller's big band tune "In the Mood" boomed from the speaker. I could feel the music sparking in the air. It was completely terrifying. I don't know if there's a term for this condition but there should be: the childhood fear of jazz from an old radio . . . I was literally unable to move. The song and the radio were cooking me alive. Finally, like someone dying in a dream, I managed to make my feet move. I backed away and ran.

I raced into the hot afternoon and worked my way blindly down the street. The neighborhood seemed ancient. The houses were all Victorian temples—they rose like gray cliffs in my diminished view. I couldn't see the particulars. There could have been dogs or people but I didn't see them. I only saw the colors and shadows of the old street.

I walked for a long time. I heard the wind everywhere above me.

It was as if the neighborhood died along with my grandfather. There were no children.

Sometimes a car passed with a whisper.

I sat under a tree and smelled decaying leaves and grass.

I thought of the radio playing back in my grandmother's parlor and imagined that it was still shaking and pouring out its hideous music. I remembered the radio's dreadful green eye.

I don't know why I was sent to live with my grandmother in that Dickensian place. My parents fought. They lived in the everlasting stress of alcohol abuse. My grandmother's house was immense and I suppose that my mother thought I would be out of sight and out of mind. I'm certain that my blindness was a factor. There were no children in the neighborhood. My mother would have imagined this as a plus—I could stay inside. I could wander from room to room.

One night, unable to sleep, I climbed the front stairs and stopped on the first landing. I pulled two balustrades from the railing of the stairs. Once they were removed I had easy access to the back of the grandfather clock that stood in a curve of the staircase. The clock had a louvered panel in the back, and with the hole I had opened in the railing I could put my head right into the machinery of the thing.

I heard chains raise and lower the iron weights. They had a vocabulary. The rising chain said *watch, watch, watch, watch.*

The lowered chain said *lucky, lucky, lucky.*

Something in the trim of the chains was out of kilter, and as they rose or fell the weights would swing and tap the glass that fronted the clock's lower body. The weights tapped the glass like raindrops.

I liked my perch at midnight. I took away the spindles from the banister and pulled aside the louvered portal and probed the secrets of the clock. The rising chain was near its zenith and the tension as it lifted the weights changed the pitch of its secret talk. It said *lucky,* but the chain spoke fast like a boy with thin arms carrying jugs of water.

There was a click from the center of the gearbox. It was like the tip of a needle tapping a dish.

Then came the sound of wings, a stirring of parts, hidden life rose into the air. A complaint of thin metal . . . old gears shuddered . . . dark fingers grabbed and clutched . . . the mahogany shivered . . . spoons clattered . . . All the clock's parts were arguing at once . . . the chimes stirred with a sound of bedsprings . . . the hammers reared back . . .

The chimes were violent, rising, shaking.

Both the glass and wood of the clock's casement and the bones of my ears were stunned.

I felt my way back to bed with my ears still ringing.

After supper I tried to get my grandmother to talk.

"What about the old days?" I asked as we sat on the porch in the growing twilight.

She was in a wicker chair and sipping lemonade.

Suddenly she said, "Your grandfather who you never knew, he had to save your mother from a wildcat one night."

She stopped for a moment and turned her chair toward me.

"That was when your mother was about the age you are now," she said.

"We were at the farm near Gilmanton, and there was a screened porch where your mother and your Aunt Muriel were sleeping on army cots. We always had lots of porcupines at that place so you really couldn't sleep outdoors. It was better if you slept on the porch. Anyway, in the middle of the night your grandfather heard a wildcat scream. It sounded like it was close to the house so he got up and found his rifle and went downstairs."

My grandmother had a way of talking that suggested irritation with every sentence. She certainly didn't want any interruptions.

"Anyway, when he got downstairs he saw the wildcat was up in the rafters right over your mother and your Aunt Muriel."

She sipped her lemonade and added for effect, "You can't shoot a wildcat if it's right above someone. And besides, there was a kerosene lantern right beside your mother's bed."

"What happened?" I asked. She'd stopped her story momentarily. She lit her cigarette.

"Your grandfather rushed into the room with a mop in his hand and waved it like a baseball bat and pushed open the screen door and waved that mop. And the cat leapt out the door."

In the coming years I would grow to believe my grandmother's family stories were embellished, but at seven I was mesmerized. I loved her yarns about my dynamite-loving grandfather who according to family legend blew up an outhouse just for the sheer hell of it. One night when he could no longer stand the noise of the porcupines rocking in the wicker chairs on the front porch, he came storming out with his gun aiming to shoot them. But the porcupines scurried in all directions as he struggled with the safety on the gun. Eventually he chased one into a utility shed and fired as it retreated behind a metal bean pot. The bullet ricocheted and struck my grandfather in the head. Everyone in the family agreed it was just a flesh wound. He bandaged his head and went about his business. The porcupine died under the floor of the toolshed and my grandfather spent a day pulling up floorboards while enduring the terrible stink of a dead animal, and of course the porcupine was under the last board he ripped from the floor. My grandmother loved this story. "He almost passed out in that hot little shack," she said. The man's suffering still ardently pleased her.

7. Tchaikovsky

◆

When I came home from my grandmother's I went directly to the hospital for eye surgery. I don't remember much about the explanations I received from my parents. It seemed like one minute I was listening to the gears of a clock and then I was in a hospital bed.

The night ward was a corridor of footsteps. I heard nurses and doctors walking on the linoleum and I pulled my sheet over my head.

When the doctor appeared he caught me by surprise. His shoes made no sound at all. He pulled back my sheets without warning and stood and looked down on me in silence.

He addressed himself to people I couldn't see as I lay in the fetal position and held my breath. This was my first experience of being described for others. The doctor refered to me as "this boy" or "this particular case" and the people behind him took notes. I could hear the pencils moving over paper.

When he was through the doctor departed without a word and his retinue followed in silent obedience. I could hear their voices murmuring in the corridor as they walked to another room.

I remember one other sound from the hospital: children weeping in the night.

After the surgery I wore bandages on my eyes.

My father read aloud to me from *The Adventures of Tom Sawyer* and I imagined Huck and Tom running blindfolded through the cave as they tried to elude Injun Joe.

My father with his slight Finnish accent was a wonderful reader. Unlike the American dads, he put emphasis and musicality into his words. He made voices for the different characters.

He looked up from the book and told me not to rub my bandages in a low voice, the voice of a Scandinavian troll.

He tried to read in the voice of a young girl and it sounded like an old woman and it was funny.

He howled when Tom must have his tooth pulled.

When he finished reading I lay on the chaise lounge in the garden and listened to the crickets.

The crickets made lively ripples of music. They sounded settled in the late afternoon sunlight. The crickets who never fell asleep.

I didn't like going outside with my bandages but my father decided it was a good moment to take me to the circus.

We stood beside the lion tamer's cage. The lions made a sound not unlike the pigs in the university's barn, a dry coughing that didn't sound very ferocious.

I fidgeted with the bandages. Adults, friends of my parents, or strangers, all had ways of suggesting that I was terribly unfortunate. "How did he get those bandages on his face?" said a woman who rang up our groceries. "Maybe there will be a small miracle!" said our postman. Walking through the circus tent with the bandages was like wandering a moonlit road. I imagined the lions were surveying me. They grunted like sows. They snorted in secret communication. They were decidedly unlion-like. They sounded fat and bored. I pressed my face to the bars of the cage.

We walked arm in arm, my father and I. I heard cage doors being opened. Doors being slammed. A man carried pails of water, the water slopping. Pulleys were like the wheels of a slow cart. There was a hum of ropes . . . Wind pushed the giant tent. All around us was the rank odor of canvas and dirty hay.

Clowns were climbing in and out of an old touring car. The motor chugged. The clowns were practicing their act: a dozen men like Keystone Kops threw themselves repeatedly into an open flivver. "Can we watch you practice?" my father asked, and a clown with a baritone voice who saw my bandaged face said, "What became of him?" My father later told me his accent was Russian. "What became of him?" I can hear the question to this day, forty years later. "Eye surgery," my father said. "Please stay," said the Russian clown. We stood at the edge of their mayhem. Their trousers ripped like flimsy sheets. Flat oversized rubber shoes slapped against the floor; slapped against the tin sides of the car; slapped against the backsides of lurching clowns who hung precariously from other clowns.

Of course I knew none of this at the moment. My father would describe their antics later as we drove home. At the moment of their leaping in that red wind I heard their groans, their innumerable gasps and curses.

The circus would open tomorrow. The lions kept snorting as if they were exhausted. The clowns sounded like birds hitting a window.

My father leaned close. "Don't rub your bandages," he said.

At night I listened to Tchaikovsky on the radio in my parents' living room. *Swan Lake* took over my heart. I could see flowers hanging over the water and a bird gliding all alone at the end of summer. I clutched a pillow so as not to rub my bandages. I was instantly in love with the music and I hunched into it.

I asked my parents to buy the record and they did. I listened to *Swan Lake* nearly a hundred times.

When my bandages came off my father took me to hear a symphony orchestra. The concert was held in the university's old field house, a building with a dirt floor and high windows and wooden bleachers.

Our seats were very close to the musicians. Though I couldn't see the orchestra I could see the gleam of horns moving, the sudden flashes of light.

The orchestra was so loud I clutched my ears. The horns exploded around us.

Before long I was crying. I couldn't control myself and wept hysterically as the great horns shook the air.

My father asked if my eyes were hurting me. I kept weeping. I didn't know how to tell him there were notes all around us that meant more than the words I could speak. I was inside it: I was Tchaikovsky's somehow. And of course I couldn't answer. I was afraid to interrupt all those dark horns.

8. *Transistor Radio, 1962*

———◆———

The girl across the street suddenly had a transistor radio.

She waved it above her head and used the word "portable."

"It's the size," she said, "of a deck of playing cards."

The first thing to jump out of Ann Robinson's radio in my presence was "Bring It on Home to Me" by Sam Cooke. The song swayed or the man did. Sam Cooke was up high. And he was sad. And his voice was lighter than lace.

Sam Cooke remains the king of pop-music loneliness for me. Others may substitute Patsy Cline or Hank Williams Sr. or Ray Charles. In any event you know it when you hear it for the first time. The sound has a thickness, like the fatness of certain flowers, and the sadness is redolent, you swear it has a fragrance. And your blood travels for a moment on the back of someone else's song.

And so I went home and begged for my own transistor radio.

My head filled with the Isley Brothers, Bobby Vee, the Drifters, Roy Orbison.

I loved the song titles best: "Your Nose Is Going to Grow"; "Venus in Blue Jeans"; "Shadrack" . . .

There was "Al Di La' " by Emilio Pericoli . . .

"All Alone Am I"—Brenda Lee . . .

"Beechwood 4-5789"—the Marvelettes . . .

"Big Girls Don't Cry"—the 4 Seasons . . .

"Bongo Stomp"—Little Joey . . .

"Bristol Twistin' Annie"—the Dovells . . .

"The Cha-Cha-Cha"—Bobby Rydell . . .

"The Cinnamon Cinder"—the Pastel Six . . .

"Crying in the Rain"—the Everly Brothers . . .

"Don't Go Near the Indians"—Rex Allen . . .

"The Duke of Earl"—Gene Chandler . . .

"My Boomerang Won't Come Back"—Charlie Drake . . .

"Summertime, Summertime"—the Jamies . . .

"She Can't Find Her Keys"—Paul Peterson . . .

I loved the hiss between the stations. The radio's plastic dial was inexact and it took a little finesse to get a signal. I learned to identify the songs as they played: "I Fall to Pieces," Patsy Cline; "Michael (Row the Boat Ashore)," the Highwaymen; "Cryin'," Roy Orbison; "Runaway," Del Shannon; "Pony Time," Chubby Checker; "Wheels," the String-a-Longs; "Raindrops," Dee Clark; "Take Good Care of My Baby," Bobby Vee; "(Will You Love Me) Tomorrow," the Shirelles; "Hit the Road, Jack," Ray Charles; "Shop Around," the Miracles; "The Boll Weevil Song," Brook Benton; "Ya Ya," Lee Dorsey . . .

The music was outlandish. Every singer was brokenhearted though I hadn't a clue as to why this should be so. But I loved it. The songs were filled with tears—unborn tears, future tears, solo tears . . .

I turned off the radio and held my breath and listened to crickets singing from all directions.

I turned on the radio and heard Dee Clark's "Raindrops." It was the voice of a man standing on tiptoe and reaching for something sweet.

I turned off the radio and heard this tree and that grass and this soft ticking of tangled branches far above.

Radio on. "Take Good Care of My Baby" by Bobby Vee . . . I was still small enough to take "baby" literally. Why is this man giving away his baby?

Radio off.

A fussy crow scolded the whole world. If he had arms he'd be waving them. He'd be standing in the middle of the street.

Radio on.

"Breakin' In a Brand New Broken Heart"—Connie Francis . . .

Radio off.

The first leaves falling at the end of summer. Pine wind . . .

Radio.

"Please Stay" by the Drifters . . .

The radio became my tutor. I was a student of loneliness.

Something was going on out there. People with impossibly beautiful voices were crying. Connie Francis was crying. The boys and girls were crying under stars.

Yes. There was plenty of heartache to go around.

It was a green day. My eyes took in a tapestry of woven colors, green shade, dark stones, impossibly bright yellow sparks of sun between trees. I lay flat on my back and listened to Elvis Presley. He was singing a song called "Little Sister" and even Elvis was sad.

Poor Elvis.

9. Telescopes

In the late summer of 1963 my father moved our family to Albany, New York, where he took a job working on one of Governor Nelson Rockefeller's pet projects—the expansion of New York's state university system.

We moved into a suburban housing development where every home looked alike and where no two families stayed for more than a year. All the fathers worked for Bell Telephone or Niagara Mohawk Power and Electric. Everyone was on the move.

I wore my earpiece and listened at night to radio stations from across the nation and knew that the whole country was moving fast. The Beach Boys sang about "Surfin' USA" and there were dozens of songs about cars and roads.

It's strange how sometimes as a kid you can understand abstract things. One night I heard a woman on the radio tell the announcer that she loved his program so much she was planning to have a radio in her coffin along with extra batteries so she could tune in after she died. Call-in programs were just becoming popular and I felt the sadness of the business. The radio had a kind of desperation about it and I could feel this. I could tell that the radio was taking the place of something more important though I didn't know for sure what that might be. But I knew enough to think of that woman planning her radio burial as a thing that was both ghastly and ridiculous.

Still I clung to songs. "My Boyfriend's Back"; "Sukiyaki"; "He's So Fine"; "Rhythm of the Rain" . . . Then John Kennedy was dead and I was back to wearing bandages on my eyes, having managed to poke myself with a screwdriver while playing in the garage. I sat beside the television and listened to the hooves of the horses as they pulled Kennedy's caisson to the cemetery. The funerary drumbeats were stirring and doleful. The marine band played "For Those in Peril on the Sea" and I felt along with the rest of the nation a bereavement none of us had known before. My father wept while he watered the lawn. "It's worse than when FDR died," my mother said.

This moment predictably enough turned me inward. Of course tens of thousands of the nation's children were traumatized by the president's death, but in my case the introspective hours became a fixation. Years later in therapy I would understand that the president's murder caused a nervous reaction in my eight-year-old mind. I was wearing telescopic spectacles in November of 1963—they were oversized bubble-shaped glasses that were designed to assist me with reading the chalkboard in school. The glasses didn't work because in addition to my retinal damage I had little or no muscular control over my eyes. When I stared through the telescopic lenses my eyes jumped uncontrollably and I saw only light and darkness.

But a kid who sat next to me—I'll call him Glenn—said quite loudly, "Well doesn't he look like Oswald?" We were at recess and Glenn pointed at my glasses. "Yeah, Oswald used telescopes just like that to shoot Kennedy!"

Glenn had hoped to start a chant of "Oswald, Oswald!" But

no one joined him and the moment fizzled. But I was tunneling into a synthetic world of radio waves with a new urgency. I thought of that woman who wanted to be buried with her radio. I wondered if they'd bury me with my telescopes.

For company I had my grandmother's 78 rpm recordings of Caruso. I sat in my suburban living room playing opera arias. I loved everything about those records: the deep red of the RCA Victor labels, the speed of the 78s on the turntable, the hollow sound of the old-fashioned recordings that were made in the years before the introduction of the electric microphone. During the recording sessions Caruso sang into a paper horn that was connected to a diaphragm and stylus. The vibrations of his voice carved the grooves in the master disk. While Caruso sang the orchestra was situated forty to fifty feet behind the tenor, and on the records the accompaniment always sounded weak—as if the instruments were played underwater. I loved the anemic bleating of the horns and the desperate strings of the violins. My favorite record was the aria from Gounod's *Faust*, "Salut! Demeure chaste et pure"—the violins on the recording were pitiful. Caruso's voice saved the orchestra because he had raw power and there was something in his baritonal tenor that the primitive recording apparatus liked. And then there was the high C that shivered from the electric speaker of my Westinghouse portable record player—a sustained and thrilling note that comes near the end of the aria. That particular high C is considered by many opera buffs to be the greatest high C ever sung because it has a painful artistry about it. One can think of it as a tenor's high note rendered in the manner of a blues singer. Faust's love is doomed even as he soars. I listened to that old record over and over again in November and December of 1963.

Predictably the neighborhood kids made fun of me. Listening to Massenet couldn't be explained and it did no good to play the aria "O Souverain" from *Le Cid*—trying to get any of them to listen to the music was just an admission of my ultimate dork-ishness. I wore telescopes. I knew Lee Harvey Oswald person-ally. I played ancient opera records, and worst of all, I would sing along in French. When I listened to those records I was back in New Hampshire in the attic and in a way I was also back in the woods.

One night the telephone rang and I raced to get it. My par-ents often praised me for my good phone manners, which meant that although I received no calls of my own they were pleased to have me answer the phone. I knew right away that I was talking to the governor of New York because Nelson Rockefeller's voice was pure gravel. Then, having asked for my father, he thought for a second and inquired how I was doing. He didn't know me. He probably asked all kids that question. I said I was listening to Caruso records. "Really?" said the governor. "I love Caruso! I grew up listening to him! My mother knew him! Good for you!"

I knew the joy of not having to say a word.

It was around this time that I discovered the pleasure of sim-ply standing still on the street.

I found that I could stop anywhere—bring to a close the walk-ing I was doing and the thinking that went with it—and suddenly the ambient noise of the neighborhood would open around me. The ordinary street outside our suburban house was surprisingly beautiful with all its fractions of living. There were little reports of living going on in every quadrant. A car slid by with its win-dows rolled down and a radio voice said, "You can whip them into shape with . . ." And then the car was out of hearing range, the voice dwindling into fuzzed vocables. You can whip them into shape with . . . with the pope's tennis racket, with the world's longest strand of spaghetti . . . I stood still and a man's voice came from across the street—there was a sound of something heavy and metallic dropped on concrete. "That's the end of that," I heard him say. He was a man with a trash can. I imagined that he had thrown away all the crucial paperwork of his life—that's the end of that—no more birth certificate, marriage license, dental records, children's report cards, vaccination certificates, tax returns, baptism records, insurance claims, dog tags, man tags, rag tags—"Any rags, any bones, any bottles today?"—I heard the voice of Groucho Marx imitating the ragpickers on the Lower East Side of New York City—I'd been watching the Marx Brothers on television—the movies were perfect for a blind kid . . . all lingua subversica—the ragpicker must be notified—there's a good can over here on (insert name of street—any town in the world). . . I was standing still. Whip them into shape. Throw away your life. A woman with two poodles walked by. "Did you lose something?" she asked. Why would a boy be standing still? Before I could answer she spoke to one of her dogs: "Leave the worm alone, Giselle!" "No," I told her, "I'm just listening." "Listening?" she said with a note of disbelief. Her poodles were prancing. She decided to keep walking.

Airplane, propeller-driven. Slow as a bumblebee. I wondered if it was trailing a banner. "Whip them into shape . . ." A door opened in a nearby house. It slammed shut. Footsteps. Then the footsteps stopped. I expected to hear a car engine starting up. No car engine. Where did the maker of footsteps disappear to? He climbed up a rope ladder into the sky. Climbed aboard the circling plane.

The ordinary street was as weird and lovely as the mind itself. All one had to do was stop.

I didn't know who I might explain this to. I wondered if Rockefeller would be interested. I thought of us sitting together and listening to Caruso. I'd tell him that French poodles eat earthworms. We'd listen to Faust.

10. Pills

———◆———

I could hear my mother in the night. She mixed pills in the kitchen. She dropped pills on the linoleum. They fell to the floor like dropped buttons. The floor would squeak as she walked in tight circles, sometimes bending to pick up fallen capsules.

I heard ice drop into her glass. My mother, alive on whiskey and barbiturates . . .

And then she was too hot and the windows went up. And then she had to move the furniture, climb up high, there was a speck on the ceiling. She would stand on a rickety table and wash the ceiling with her moistened index finger. Or else she'd move the furniture because she'd lost something long ago—a wristwatch, a paperback novel . . .

From the age of ten or so I would lie awake and listen to her moving restlessly about the house. I wondered what she was hearing? In my teenage years when I experimented with drugs I listened to rock and roll, hoping to glean nuances of meaning from the dialogue of shouts and rhythm. But my mother listened to no music. And so I must imagine that her pills had their own tiny and operatic recitatives. These must have been ironical, bitter, or jeering . . . Or else they produced the sound of wind in a trellis and the whispers of a child in hiding. Who knows the misery of others? I know she walked around the house almost nightly. And I know that dull matter, spoons and shelves and all the other homely oddments, would clatter to the floor or refuse to help her.

The secret of pills is the secret of the Sphinx. The pill taker is the Eleusinian candidate waiting in tall grass. Soon it will come: verdure, sympathy of thought, the bright jellyfish of the over-mind, love and love rising in the spine and tipping the scales of mind.

I was awake. I now know that being unable to sleep is a coefficient of visual loss. Many blind people lie awake in a weird radio-astronomy of concentrated thinking. And down below me in the cold kitchen my mother walked around in her small clattering way. *I'm here*, said her footsteps. *I'm here*. Such a midnight sound . . .

11. The Voice of the Dark

———◆———

I was barely home from school. My shirt was torn at the shoulder because a tall and oddly stinky boy named Jerry had ripped the seam while shouting, "Let's court-martial him! Let's 'brand' him for being a deserter! He's a traitor to our country!"

With that five boys from the sixth grade piled on top of me. I'd been sitting alone under a tree and listening to the red-winged blackbirds. The birds sounded like plastic combs scraped by thumbs. Now Jerry and the boys were holding me down in the grass, punching my arms, tearing my sleeves, singing a television sitcom theme song that had something to do with branding a man who was a traitor to the Union army. My glasses flew away into the underbrush. My spine buckled.

They sang on top of me in unison, like the Hitler Youth.

"What do you do when you're branded
And you know you're a man?"

"Aw shit," said Jerry, "He's too skinny for branding!" They took to punching each other and then they ran away in a kind of scrum, slapping each other and laughing as they disappeared.

I learned how to reclaim the world after these moments by entering a self-made audible environment. In my room at home I listened to Talking Books for the Blind on long-playing records from the Library of Congress. While a book played on one record player I'd listen to classical music on another machine. I heard, simultaneously, the songs of Hector Berlioz and chapters from *Huckleberry Finn*. I loved Berlioz's treatment of the death of Ophelia, the soprano and the pianist sinking in a wholly Romantic way. The piano poured gentle waves over the drowning girl. The Berlioz songs were pastries for the ear and I loved them because they were equally sincere and crazy. Kids do get these things. In *The Adventures of Huckleberry Finn,* Mark Twain presents Huck both loving and mocking the draw-ings of a death-obsessed girl, Emmeline Grangerford, who in fact dies early from a fever. I loved that section of *Huck Finn* and played it over several times. Huck describes the dead girl's pictures this way:

> *There was some that they called crayons, which one of the daughters which was dead made her own self when she was only fifteen years old. They was different from any pictures I ever see before; blacker, mostly, than is common. One was a woman in a slim black dress, belted small under the armpits, with bulges like a cabbage in the middle of the sleeves, and a large black scoop-shovel bonnet with a black veil, and white slim ankles crossed about with black tape, and very wee black slippers, like a chisel, and she was leaning pensive on a tombstone on her right elbow, under a weeping willow, and her other hand hanging down her side holding a white handkerchief and a reticule, and underneath the picture it said "Shall I Never See Thee More Alas." Another one was a young lady with her hair all combed up straight to the*

top of her head, and knotted there in front of a comb like a chair-back, and she was crying into a handkerchief and had a dead bird laying on its back in her other hand with its heels up, and under-neath the picture it said "I Shall Never Hear Thy Sweet Chirrup More Alas." There was one where a young lady was at a window looking up at the moon, and tears running down her cheeks; and she had an open letter in one hand with black sealing-wax show-ing on one edge of it, and she was mashing a locket with a chain to it against her mouth, and underneath the picture it said "And Art Thou Gone Yes Thou Art Gone Alas." These was all nice pictures, I reckon, but I didn't somehow seem to take to them, because if ever I was down a little they always give me the fan-tods. Everybody was sorry she died, because she had laid out a lot more of these pictures to do, and a body could see by what she had done what they had lost. But I reckoned, that with her dispo-sition, she was having a better time in the graveyard. She was at work on what they said was her greatest picture when she took sick, and every day and every night it was her prayer to be allowed to live till she got it done, but she never got the chance. It was a picture of a young woman in a long white gown, stand-ing on the rail of a bridge all ready to jump off, with her hair all down her back, and looking up to the moon, with the tears run-ning down her face, and she had two arms folded across her breast, and two arms stretched out in front, and two more reach-ing up towards the moon—and the idea was, to see which pair would look best and then scratch out all the other arms; but, as I was saying, she died before she got her mind made up, and now they kept this picture over the head of the bed in her room, and every time her birthday come they hung flowers on it. Other times it was hid with a little curtain. The young woman in the picture had a kind of a nice sweet face . . .

I was alone in my suburban bedroom, chewing black licorice, listening to Twain and Berlioz. I could still smell Jerry's sweat on my torn sleeve: it was an odor like apples and methane. The record players scratched and delivered their multiple voices. After the drowning of Ophelia the Berlioz record offered up a song called "La Captive" that began: "If I were not a captive, / I would have loved this land . . ." I had no idea what the song was actually about. But it was filled with an abundance of misery and sweetness.

One afternoon after listening to Caruso singing "Core 'ngrato" I caught the end of the *Four O'Clock Movie* on television. The film was *The Great Caruso* starring Mario Lanza. What an amazing thing! My operatic hero was there before me, the subject of a Hollywood tearjerker. I'd tuned in at the end of the movie and Caruso was deathly ill. He was backstage at the Brooklyn Academy of Music with blood streaming from his mouth. Mario Lanza was spitting blood into a towel but even so he was shoving aside his entourage. He was going back onstage. The crowd was calling.

I leaned close to the television and Mario Lanza sang "Celeste Aida."

Then the Great Caruso was dead. In the movie he died like Gary Cooper in the role of Lou Gehrig. Caruso was the luckiest man in the world. They buried him with the kings of Italy.

The next day at four o'clock I tuned in again, hoping for something musical. Instead I heard John Wayne vow to kill Montgomery Clift. Then there was the tremendous thunder of a cattle stampede.

I could tell at once there was something beautiful here: two men vowing to kill one another and the cattle gone wild.

John Wayne talked like a bandsaw. He pushed his syllables with a firm resolve that sounded flat but was sharp at the edges.

I knew this voice because I'd practiced it myself. It's the voice of all kids who grow up alone. You talk to the dark. You take it in and spit it out and you just decide you know what you're talking about because no one else is ever going to help you. And the cattle bellowed behind him as he vowed to kill Montgomery Clift.

12. The Sound of My Mother's Body

———◆———

There were gunshots and then there were Indians and more gunshots. Then there were familiar voices: Walter Brennan was the old man in charge of the ramshackle cook wagon. John Wayne was going mad on the cattle drive. His voice was like a soft fever. Montgomery Clift was young and full of wholesomeness. Walter Brennan knew about men going crazy on cattle drives, though his wisdom was ignored because he sounded like a parrot.

I ate Swedish rye crackers with pickled herring and listened to John Wayne talk like a madman. His voice was all thistles and bourbon. He was swaying in the bodega, and leaning on his every syllable. For a week the local TV station showed John Wayne movies at four: *The Searchers, Rio Bravo, The Alamo*. I liked how John Wayne could hesitate and then fall into a mood: playing Davy Crockett, he would suddenly admire the branches of a tree. It was his way of telling Flaca, played by Linda Cristal, that he knew he was going to die.

It was "la mort de Crockett"—a fit song for Berlioz.

In the schoolyard even stinky Jerry admired my ability to imitate "the Duke." I had the catch in the voice, that Puritan bafflement in the face of true emotion. I talked like a madman. "Them your shoes?" I said to Jerry, then added: "A man shouldn't die in boots like those." Jerry and the playground boys ate this up.

Around this time my mother had an accident while entering a supermarket. The automatic door failed as she was crossing the threshold and the full weight of the slamming door struck her elbow. She fell against a window with a terrible crack. I was just a few steps ahead of her and I heard the sequenced sounds of the door and elbow and then her torso hitting the plate glass. I was fascinated by radio sound effects and knew that the noise of her body hitting the window sounded exactly like a dropped bag of apples. Then there was a gasp—her gasp, different from any cry I'd ever heard. When the mallet strikes nerves just right, we are all strangers and all simultaneously familiar. My poor mother! Then I heard a man's voice call out: "Hey Frank! Tie the damned door open again!" And there were strangers, women mostly, saying "What happened to her?" and the supermarket manager exclaiming that this had happened before and he was sorry. My mother was helped to her feet by the driver of a bread truck. Mr. Wonder Bread to the rescue.

Now she was suing the supermarket and I was going to be her chief witness.

I was so excited! I practiced my John Wayne accents while imagining myself on the stand. And then my mother's lawyer came to our house and my role in the proceedings was discussed. We sat in our living room and the lawyer snapped open his briefcase and extracted a clean pad of paper. I was immediately thrilled. Jerry and the boys made fun of me almost daily because I insisted on carrying an old leather briefcase to school.

It was a fetish. It said that I would be someone in the world beyond the valley.

The lawyer made notes with a fountain pen that sounded like a bird's feet in the leaves. He wrote while my mother recounted her story. She was wearing a sling and described the elbow surgery she would most likely need. She had some kind of unresponsive fracture. The lawyer asked her lots of medical questions and scratched with the pen. I didn't know it, but an important moment in my life was about to occur. Like so many signature moments, it would happen without any drama. It would happen in a small suburban living room about fifteen miles south of Albany, New York.

The lawyer spoke about a hypothetical trial. He said that the problem with my mother's case was that her only witness was blind. "I know Stephen heard everything," he said, "but the lawyers for the supermarket will say that he can't be reliable because he couldn't see what was happening."

My strange and often silent mother, that is, silent where my blindness was concerned, suddenly said: "He's got better ears than Leonard Bernstein and a memory for detail that would impress Houdini. So you ought to talk to him."

And then I was in the cold, clear sky of facts, my favorite place. The lawyer was asking me about listening. I told him what I'd heard in the supermarket and what the store manager had said about the door being broken again. Then the lawyer asked me if I was sure about what I'd heard. I told him how I treated every day like a requiem.

"A what?" said the lawyer, his pen suddenly still.

"A requiem. You know, a musical mass that's performed when someone famous dies. You can think of a whole day as a kind of musical pattern. Do you know the parts of a requiem?"

The lawyer didn't know.

"There's the opening, *in memoria aeterna*—it sets the mood. Then there's the *Dies Irae* and the *Tuba mirum* and the *Judex ergo* . . ."

I told him about the sound my mother's body made when it hit the window.

I told him about the creation of sound effects in a radio studio. I said that with your eyes closed you could confuse one noise with another unless you really knew the character of a sound. I told him that a snipe rising from the grass sounds different from a pheasant. I was flat out happy, talking about the wilderness of noises and the hours in a day. I was the kid the others liked to smack around. I was the kid the others couldn't resist liking. I said that Mario Lanza was no Caruso. I said that John Wayne was no Davy Crockett. I said that in all likelihood the real Davy Crockett probably sounded like Walter Brennan.

The lawyer put his pad of paper back in his briefcase and snapped it shut. He said that I could most certainly take the stand. He said suddenly, and with the kind of earnestness that all children hope to receive from adults: "You are the finest listener I've ever met. I have learned something here."

He shook my hand.

I was part of some still-unnamed tribe. But I was in the village. I was officially something.

I never did have to take the stand. The supermarket settled with my mother out of court. But I was a designated listener, and the status this conferred was, at least to me, the equivalent of a recognizable athletic skill.

13. Paradise Lost

———◆———

When I was fourteen, I discovered the sound of iniquity on a long-playing record for the blind from the Library of Congress. I listened to *Paradise Lost*, and sometimes after hours of playing the story of Satan I'd walk to the driveway's edge and feel the elaborate work of sunlight and wind and imagine, the way only a teenager can, the falling of Satan in a blackness so pure you could feel it in the bones of your face.

I'd discovered, without knowing it, the difference between speaking and being. This is what listening is, true listening, the lonely but open mind. I'd discovered the gift of Milton: the soul's path is in the ear—not in the mirror.

The needle worked its way through long grooves of spoken words. Outside, October sunlight kept trusting God's plan.

Upstairs my mother slept with the shades drawn. She drank too much.

The needle scratched. And John Milton promised a flight straight toward badness:

To do aught good never will be our task,
But ever to do ill our sole delight,

As being the contrary to his high will
Whom we resist. If then his Providence
Out of our evil seek to bring forth good,
Our labor must be to pervert that end,
And out of good still to find means of evil;
Which oft-times may succeed, so as perhaps
Shall grieve him, if I fail not, and disturb
His inmost counsels from thir destin'd aim.

I listened beside a window and just outside the last of the autumn crickets sang. I thought of their song as a little chorus of the good. Somewhere above me a hornet worked its way along the ceiling. In the meantime Satan passed through the kingdom of the dead on his way to the Garden of Eden.

I'd entered the netherworlds of John Milton by accident. A substitute music teacher appeared one day in my Albany, New York, junior high school. He was wildly implausible: a Miltonist from Mississippi, nearly seventy, with a voice like Red Barber. He didn't know a thing about music. He stood before a wide room that was filled with band instruments and a dozen or so teenage boys. He stood stock-still before us. He stared us down. And we, who had been writhing in our seats, we stopped moving. Then he recited:

Of Man's First Disobedience, and the Fruit
Of that Forbidden Tree, whose mortal taste
Brought Death into the World, and all our woe,
With loss of Eden, till one greater Man
Restore us, and regain the blissful Seat,
Sing Heav'nly Muse, that on the secret top
Of Oreb, or of Sinai, didst inspire
That Shepherd, who first taught the chosen Seed,

In the Beginning how the Heav'ns and Earth
Rose out of Chaos: Or if Sion Hill
Delight thee more, and Siloa's Brook that flow'd
Fast by the Oracle of God; I thence
Invoke thy aid to my advent'rous Song,
That with no middle flight intends to soar
Above th' Aonian Mount, while it pursues
Things unattempted yet in Prose or Rhyme.

The room was hot. It was early afternoon. All the boys had eaten too much lunch. Each of us was toxic with hormones and our dramas of digestion. Now here was this voice, this presence really, unforeseen, peculiar, at once both soft and hard—a voice from the seventeenth century, a voice that could pronounce words like "blissful" and give them true shape—a voice that could easily suggest contempt for middle flight. He talked and I was gone somehow. The whole room was gone. We were in the smoke of jargon. And he went on reciting. Until we began to sense that something was vastly different about this hour after lunch.

He stopped and looked us over. No one said a thing. There was only the sound of traffic outside on Washington Avenue.

"That's *Paradise Lost* by John Milton," he said, "a blind poet from England in the 1600s. He knew the affairs of good and evil in humankind."

He knew how to say "affairs" and "humankind"—the lilt that comes with half a dipthong, that circular softness in the vowel.

He also could say good and evil and mean it. He was perfectly strange and he had our attention for a little while. He was not of our lives.

Soon enough we would consider him crazy.

It was 1969. Our lives were pure play. We listened to Jim

Morrison and Jimi Hendrix. The high school next door was shut down at least once a week by a bomb scare.

This man named Mercer who sounded as though he had stepped from the pages of *The Sound and the Fury,* this fevered man spoke about good and evil in what should have been a music class. And he read to us about the fiery circumference of hell and I'm sure that more than one of us fell asleep to that voice that hummed like bees in an orchard.

To do aught good never will be our task,
But ever to do ill our sole delight,
As being the contrary to his high will . . .

Boys love good and evil in stories, and for a time Mr. Mercer made Satan so very real that we slipped, intact, into Milton's varied planes of action and being. Outside of class we'd joke of course. We'd mime the man's gestures and wave the invisible book for emphasis. I worked on imitating his voice. I overdid it with elaborate lifts of vowels but I captured a little of the madness just as once I'd managed to imitate John Wayne gone mad on a cattle drive. That was my way. And damned if I didn't feel evil while doing it. It was a masturbatory guilt I felt. It's possible that imitation is the sincerest form of flattery, but it's also adolescent and the art is steeped in shame. And therefore it is addictive. And this is the origin of irony, and when we're really thinking we never forget the first time we understood it.

Mercer was, as previously noted, all fever. Not one of us comprehended what he was up to. What had begun as a novelty, Milton read aloud with a southern flair, became quickly a tyranny. Fourteen-year-olds know nothing of administration and lack the confidence to seek official redress, and so we sat

through two full weeks of Milton and during all that time Mr.
Mercer never once mentioned music. Soon enough he was just
another insane adult in our eyes. He read aloud and we returned
to swiveling in our chairs and cursing just below Mercer's level
of hearing. One of us practiced smoking with an unlit Pall Mall.
Mercer would sometimes stop reading and talk about the human
joy of doing evil and the higher virtues of resistance. I thought I
heard in his voice something that was of course intangible but
real, something sincere. At moments as he read I felt I was racing into space. I realized also that John Milton was indeed a
musical figure, and what's more, that Milton, or was it Mercer,
could make me feel transparent.

I found that when alone I wanted to puzzle this out. Was it
Mercer or Milton who could do this thing to me? I ordered *Paradise Lost* from the library for the blind and when it arrived in its
immense black carton I raced to my record player. I needed to
hear Milton read aloud by someone who was not Mercer, someone who was not obviously pushing his own heart around the
indifferent room.

The words from the machine came as blue and tense syllables.

Meanwhile the Adversary of God and Man,
Satan with thoughts inflam'd of highest design,
Puts on swift wings, and towards the Gates of Hell
Explores his solitary flight; sometimes
He scours the right hand coast, sometimes the left,
Now shaves with level wing the Deep, then soars
Up to the fiery concave tow'ring high.

The voice on the record was more sonorous than Mercer's, a
Brahmin voice. I saw quickly that this didn't matter. Milton could
join you with the air and with the held breath of vengeance. Old

Satan was going to fly out of Hell and mess with Man and I could go with him and feel my blood washing against the whiteness of creation. I knew that Mercer was onto something.

Years later, when I was studying the craft of poetry writing at the University of Iowa, I told the poet Donald Justice how I listened all alone to Milton on records and felt my own little soul bumping along the roof of my skull. Don was quite likely the best-read poet of his generation and he understood loneliness in childhood, and he said that only Milton could put God's breath into punctuation. I knew that Don was right: Milton holds you in the air and holds you and holds you until you feel your own pulse.

In the schoolroom, meanwhile, things were going to pieces. Mercer was determined to read us the whole of *Paradise Lost* and boys interrupted him demanding to be allowed to go to the restroom. Mercer was indignant. "Please," one boy cried, "I need to freshen my lipstick!" Mercer's voice trembled with calm. We were to use the restroom before class began. Fluorescent lights buzzed over our heads. And the legs of chairs were scraped rhythmically on the old linoleum. There was no relief for Mercer and none for us. He read on as we threw books to the floor. There was flatulence. Spitballs struck thighs and cheekbones.

Pitiable Mercer! He was in love with *Paradise Lost*—in love, learned and lost . . .

He read on in spite of us and Milton's serpent explained to Eve how he came to speak like humankind:

> *I was at first as other Beasts that graze*
> *The trodden Herb, of abject thoughts and low,*
> *As was my food, nor aught but food discern'd*
> *Or Sex, and apprehended nothing high:*
> *Till on a day roving the field, I chanc'd*

A goodly Tree far distant to behold
Loaden with fruit of fairest colors mixt,
Ruddy and Gold: I nearer drew to gaze;
When from the boughs a savory odor blown,
Grateful to appetite, more pleas'd my sense
Than smell of sweetest Fennel, or the Teats
Of Ewe or Goat dropping with Milk at Ev'n,
Unsuckt of Lamb or Kid, that tend thir play.
To satisfy the sharp desire I had
Of tasting those fair Apples, I resolv'd
Not to defer; hunger and thirst at once,
Powerful persuaders, quick'n'd at the scent
Of that alluring fruit, urg'd me so keen.

Mercer read and we cried out, repeating "savory odor blown!"
"Sex!" "Teats!" "Unsuckt!"

And Mercer's voice went on, his tone rueful, his diction numbingly precise . . .

At home I listened alone, sliding in the unhaphazard intelligence of John Milton, transformed by the weird charts of emotion and grasping at the language.

What else did I know? I'd been listening to recorded books or discovering sounds while alone from my earliest days. I could find patterns in street noises and listen at night to my mother's footsteps as she walked the house—sometimes walking until it was nearly dawn.

It was October and unseasonably hot. The Beatles sang "Come Together" and no one was together in the ambient spaces where I listened.

My father had become a college president and the dormitories at the university were firebombed the week he took office. The state police came to our house and looked through our flower garden with metal detectors. My father was in a shadow and he rarely came out. Sometimes he fought with my mother late at night. It seemed he hardly noticed her. It seemed she hated his career.

The world was cruel and driven by appetites. No one was fulfilled. Listening through walls or to the grooves of records, I was getting it—there were actions one couldn't take back. It was the difference between speaking and being. Milton's Eve didn't seem to know the difference. My classmates didn't get it either. People listened for confirmation rather than the harder things. The air outside was warm as a bath. I was alone with my ridiculous records. I could see Adam and Eve, white as bone. I played passages over again, lifting the heavy tone arm of the record machine and dropping it on the spinning record. I held my nearly disembodied head and sometimes I even held my breath.

Then Mercer was gone. He disappeared from class the same week the New York Mets defeated the Baltimore Orioles in the World Series, and accordingly the boys didn't have any leftover curiosity about what might have happened to him. He was replaced by a college girl with long braids and granny glasses who encouraged us to bring our favorite pop-music records to class for group discussion. We were going to listen for confirmation. I'd begun to figure out what people meant by "relevance" and I knew I wasn't up to it.

One kid played Simon & Garfunkel's "The Sounds of Silence." Another guy played Sly and the Family Stone. We were free to be straightforward and hopelessly sincere. Someone played the Beatles' "Hey Jude." Soon it would be my turn to bring my favorite pop record to class and the prospect gave me "the fan-tods," as Huck Finn would say. I liked rock and roll plenty and could have produced some vintage Sam Cooke or something by the Yardbirds, but the prospect of talking about Eric Clapton was disagreeable—I knew how this would go. Someone would shout "Who's better, Clapton or Hendrix?" and things would devolve from there into a discussion of rock guitar supremacy and it would become a free-for-all.

But I was a longtime cutoff listener. I could identify the call of a purple finch without confusing him with a thrush. I enjoyed the songs of Hector Berlioz and at the same time I loved the Marx Brothers in the movie *Monkey Business*. When Harpo tries to pass himself off to French customs officials as Maurice Chevalier by brandishing Chevalier's stolen passport and wearing a Victrola on his back, well, that's art, then and now, and I was lucky enough to know it even though I was still too inexperienced to guess if I would find a way in the world of style. I knew that much. Things seen and heard are not the same.

Then it was my turn. I lugged my enormous Library of Congress talking-book record machine into school and carried it up three flights of stairs to the classroom. The voice from the speaker was deeper than Mercer's and it was gloomy. And no one laughed because the show was unanticipated. I said that Adam and Eve were now being banished from the garden because they couldn't distinguish between what they'd wanted to hear and what they already understood to be the truth.

> *So spake our Mother Eve, and Adam heard*
> *Well pleas'd, but answer'd not; for now too nigh*
> *Th' Arch-Angel stood, and from the other Hill*
> *To thir fixt Station, all in bright array*
> *The Cherubim descended; on the ground*
> *Gliding meteorous, as Ev'ning Mist*
> *Ris'n from a River o'er the marish glides,*

And gathers ground fast at the Laborer's heel
Homeward returning. High in Front advanc't,
The brandisht Sword of God before them blaz'd
Fierce as a Comet; which with torrid heat,
And vapor as the Libyan Air adust,
Began to parch that temperate Clime; whereat
In either hand the hast'ning Angel caught
Our ling'ring Parents, and to th' Eastern Gate
Let them direct, and down the Cliff as fast
To the subjected Plaine; then disappear'd.
They looking back, all th' Eastern side beheld
Of Paradise, so late thir happy seat,
Wav'd over by that flaming Brand, the Gate
With dreadful Faces throng'd and fiery Arms:
Some natural tears they dropp'd, but wip'd them soon;
The World was all before them, where to choose
Thir place of rest, and Providence thir guide:
They hand in hand with wand'ring steps and slow,
Through Eden took thir solitary way.

The needle rasped at the paper label for a moment.

I picked up the tone arm and held the record up like an Olympic discus. "There's Braille on the label because this record is for blind people," I said. "Can you imagine how solitary John Milton must have been in the days when there was no Braille and no blind person could read a book without help? He had to listen to voices. He had to figure out who was telling the truth without seeing their faces."

There was a long silence. I was in the midst of people whose ways were not my own. I was alone with the spirits of Milton and the vanished Mercer.

Then it was the next kid's turn to play a record. I sat down and listened to "Aquarius" by the Fifth Dimension.

I thought of Mercer reading aloud while the class whispered.

I liked the way he did that. I could tell that I liked it more than I at first supposed. I was comfortable in a room of words recited, brief though such visits may sometimes be.

Two

"WALKING BY EAR"

Why travel anywhere if you can't see?

— WOMAN, ANONYMOUS,
CARROLL CENTER FOR THE BLIND, BOSTON

*I haven't understood a bar of music in my life,
but I have felt it.*

— IGOR STRAVINSKY

14. Dog-Man: The Action Figure

——◆——

I have just returned from a trip that took me to many cities. I was in Chicago, New York, New Orleans, and then New York again. I should tell you up front that I am not a man—not specifically. One ought to think of me as a six-legged being for I am both a man and a dog. But of course that's not exactly right. I'm a capable blind man who travels everywhere with a trained dog. I'm told we look good together. We're simpatico. We're intuitive. Occult. We can hear everything. We think for each other. Entering the subway in Manhattan, we are a kind of centaur: man-head with dog's body . . . or is it the other way around? Maybe we have two heads. Six legs. We go very fast in the dark. I know this for certain. We go very fast beneath the city.

And so we are an "action figure."

My stepson Ross plays with plastic "action figures." These are stylized and molded supermen with lots of parts. I once called them toy soldiers and he corrected me. "Action figures," he said, "have hands that hold things." By this he meant light sabers and atomic guns and the like. One could discuss what constitutes a real action figure as opposed to a simple comic book hero. A figurine that represents Superman, for example, would not be an approved action figure since Superman doesn't carry tools or weapons. Ross's guys come equipped with rotating hands and arms. They fly about with their galactic equipage. They scowl, every one of them, each caught in a deplorable mania that comes from the stars.

Two days ago I woke early and dressed for Chicago's October rain. I had an early appointment and my dog Corky and I raced out of the old Palmer House Hilton into a great audio postcard of waterfalls and wheels and automobile horns and that thin silver whistle of the doorman who hails taxis.

I was crossing Michigan Avenue when a car ran a light and Corky pulled backward and saved us from certain injury. Then she nosed forward and got us to the far sidewalk. A crowd of people surrounded us, strangers applauding and touching man and dog to make certain we were safe. It was beautiful and I wanted to cry. I wanted to cry as I sometimes do when I get to the *Lux aeterna* in Mozart's *Requiem*. The more acute the experience, the less articulate its expression. I think Harold Pinter said that. I just swayed in the slow rain of Chicago and fought back tears. My Labrador, my big yellow soul mate, was standing on her hind legs, her forepaws on my shoulders. She was washing my face. And people stood around me and used words like "miracle" and "grace of God." One guy said I should buy the dog a beer. Someone else said that Corky was "heroic" and I should get her a steak instead.

We resumed our walk and the rain stopped and I heard the sounds you hear when the rain ends: spoked bicycle wheels spitting water, branches swaying with thickened voices . . .

We turned onto Wabash Avenue: Corky watching, man daydreaming after a near-death experience.

I was thinking about the notion those bystanders had that Corky was a hero.

A motorcycle passed on the street, its valves out of kilter, the machine badly in need of a tune-up.

I was thinking that bourgeois America loves its heroes to be modeled on images from antiquity.

I heard someone crossing the street at a run. There was the slap of his soaked sneakers.

Corky is in fact heroic, I thought, *but so is her human partner, so is the person in running shoes whose footsteps were now indistinct behind the emotionless hum of ten thousand rain-soaked tires.*

I thought of how heroism in an individual is a backward notion. If heroism means anything, it must have to do with group activity.

We stopped under the elevated tracks and a train roared over us.

Like all guide dogs, Corky is loyal, aware, and brave. *What makes her Greek*, I thought, *is her beauty. And the beauty has all to do with two-creature Eros.*

O my sweet, winged dog! We have such familiarity! We are flying over the ordinary sidewalks. To approaching pedestrians we must seem like two lamps in the heart of a cloud . . . Pollux and Castor singing their unfinished song . . . Of course there's heroism in this moment of being . . .

The trouble, I thought, *is that the public doesn't really see us as Pollux and Castor. They think the guide dog is the isolated hero. They don't view us as a team.*

I heard an indistinct jingle that didn't match the traffic. What was that? It was a thin, curved sound from far up the avenue.

I could tell it was an old sound: one of those occasional small melodies that make you think of childhood.

It came to me then: it was the sound of reindeer bells. Someone or some animal was shaking bells on Wabash.

This is the flowing world, I thought, *with all its potentialities.*

There was a cheerful rising and tapering of reindeer bells, a sound I first heard long ago in Finland.

We walked some more. I heard a stonemason hammering at some broken steps.

We glided around a set of bedsprings left out by workers from a hotel that was being renovated. A boy who sounded like he was around ten years old was jumping on the coils, an activity that made a green and golden noise.

He liked the dog. I liked the bedsprings. He told me about the hotel being renovated and about finding the springs. I let him hold Corky's leash. He allowed me to jump on the coils. Because I was clumsier or heavier, the springs did not make a green and golden sound for me. Instead they made an impoverished noise under my feet.

The boy watched as Corky and I continued up the sidewalk. He called out approvingly when Corky went around a basement delivery door that had been left open. I felt her caution, her body's whole intelligence signaling through the handle of her harness. She was watching and moving and I thought: *If I must be somebody . . . I will be this . . . Amitabha Buddha . . . mutual compassion makes us trusting . . . the rhythm of living flesh united in belief . . . we go places and are more real than dewdrops or suffering . . .*

I thought about trust. We're all of us weak on trust. I was being swept forward by what Santayana called "animal faith"—unreasoned joy . . .

O my dog! Together we are fast!

When I was first training with Corky some years back my friend Dave See, a veteran guide-dog trainer, told me that letting the dog navigate would free up my ability to listen.

"Once you get used to it," Dave said, "you can tell the differences between streets just by listening."

Dave was right. The music of even ordinary streets prevails. Wabash has a different music from Dearborn.

Dave was accurate, though this isn't simple. Ear travel demands effort and optimism.

The poet Yeats wrote: "The fascination of what's difficult / Has dried the sap out of my veins, and rent / Spontaneous joy and natural content / Out of my heart."

Poor Yeats! He trafficked with ghosts and disparaging prophecies. He imagined that his wife could talk with the dead. Mrs. Yeats went into trances and wrote down the words of ghosts. Predictably, as Ireland buckled with violence the poet received a vision of the cosmos collapsing into chaos. Ahead lay only darkness and human brutality.

"Terror . . ." writes Stephen King, "often arises from a pervasive sense of disestablishment; that things are in the unmaking."

Always the world is "in the unmaking." Trouble always stands ahead.

Is it possible to say that Yeats was foolish and not a fool? I think this is the case. A fool blinks, chooses physical love and trusts that darkness will take care of itself. "I am two fools, I know," wrote John Donne. "I am two fools, I know, / For loving, and for saying so / In whining poetry."

Yeats trusted language over love. Trouble with the heart's wellspring always lies that way. I side with fools: darkness takes care of itself. Fierce loving is my way in the street. Before this dog are bedsprings, broken bicycles, the stray machinery, and she moves through it all, guiding us into receptive darkness.

I traveled last week. I was in three cities over a six-day period.

I held on to my dog. My dog held on to me.

Again, I had this sense for just a moment as we walked through the French Quarter of New Orleans that we were a centaur.

She was the feet.

Then she was the head and I was the feet.

We were Dog-Man.

We sailed among unidentified objects.

We navigated a construction site and then a group of half-helpless, singing drunks.

There was an ocarina.

Things are, I thought, *in the unmaking.*

15. The Invention of the Cell Phone

———◆———

I'm listening to Felix Mendelssohn's *Songs without Words,* the music rising from a radio in my study. The pianist, William Kapell, died in a plane crash while still a young man and there's a young man's delicacy to the handling of Mendelssohn's elusive opening phrases. The music says we are still in love with our tentative thoughts; the heart's arousal is a kindness—nothing more. Outside sleet strikes at the window, a crow calls from a neighbor's yard. This is the early hour when I can still hear. All feelings are first feelings: the world is not yet constructed. The poplars in fresh snow sway in the January wind.

Kapell's recording isn't digital. It has a muted and oddly selfless quality. It's still dark outside.

"The movement is from delight to wisdom and not vice versa," says Seamus Heaney. He is talking about the moment when a poem arrives but he's also talking about hearing something new: "The felicity of a cadence, the chain reaction of a rhyme, the pleasuring of an etymology, such things can proceed happily and, as it were, autistically, in an area of mental operations cordoned off by and from the critical sense."

So first sounds are a delirium! Just now Kapell reminds me that the timbre of a piano can mimic our astonishment at being alive. This musical sensation may be the origin of tears of joy.

"In the little flowing world the tears lose meaning," writes the Estonian poet Jaan Kaplinski. The sun is not yet up and already Mendelssohn has taken me to Estonia. And there I see Jaan Kaplinski, Buddhist, linguist, poet, father. I imagine he's walking among the sparkling birch trees outside of Tartu, the old university town. I picture him in a kind of auditory hallucination: above the poet, high in the trees, the superb crows of Estonia are calling out.

Birds scurry on my roof.

The ears, I think, *are a dream we will never be rid of.*

Forget serendipity—all the luck of chance music, sound, even the most ineffable sound is permanent—a continuous wave throughout creation. *Lacrymosa dies illa . . .* And now the string theorists confirm it. We are vibrating endlessly in the present, which is also the past and future.

The radio on my desk plays Mendelssohn so sweetly I want to speak foolish, loving words to the earth—the old, dark winter earth who forgets all our proper names . . .

Yes, listening is the lonely art.

Sometimes while traveling by myself I've awakened in strange towns and heard foreign noises and languages. In those moments I am more than a little brokenhearted. I am the blind traveler who listens not merely for utility but for sustenance.

Pablo Neruda heard the salt singing in its shaker, a song of mineral anguish—the music of oceans and lost bodies. Franz Liszt heard apples muttering in a wicker basket.

There are joys in chance sounds. But there is also bewilderment.

I woke once all alone in a hotel in Raleigh, North Carolina, and listened for a long time as if I might hear the salt. I had of course been listening to tape recordings of Neruda.

At first there was a delicious vagueness to everything. The piped air forced through five hundred rooms blew above my head. It came from unknown countries and anonymous joys; it carried the exhalations of strangers though the words had been removed.

The forced air above me poured from infinity.

It occurred to me that I knew nothing. I was blind and visiting a strange town and I had no friends nearby. I was alone in a hotel listening to conditioned air. I resolved in that moment to spend my day listening in that complicated, postmodern hotel. Standing in my room, I shifted from thinking about Neruda to thoughts of Walt Whitman.

Whitman liked walking in harbors to hear the wind knock against the tackle of sailing boats. He liked the music of boats going nowhere . . . the clatter of a thousand masts like dropped spoons . . . Whitman could reconstruct a whole day from sounds remembered in sequence. This was my ambition, at least for the moment; an idea as ephemeral as a New Year's resolution.

Standing in the cavernous lobby of the hotel, I could locate the escalators by means of their hum, that lift of air like a breeze disturbing blankets at the beach. When I drew closer I could hear the whisper of rolling metal, a feverish sound.

There was a wishing well in the atrium and children threw coins. I heard their father instructing them, his deep voice like a low hanging branch. He was an American father. He wanted his children's money to land in the right place. The man was fatuous and I ignored him just to hear the coins.

I turned then and followed a corridor where there was no carpet. There was the quick staccato of a woman's heels on the tiled floor. She was a woman in a hurry. I pictured her clutching papers, late for a meeting. A woman's haste is music. Her footfalls were like a cobbler's hammer. Then she was gone.

Fluorescent lights hummed above me. Salt was singing in the shaker. Copper sang and mercury gas sang. I remembered a line from one of Robert Bly's poems: *There are murdered kings in the light bulbs outside movie theaters.* Kings of the Iron Age still howl in the flood of amperes.

I walked through a series of rooms. There was the tinkling of glassware. It was an average American hotel. No birds sang from cages. There was nothing in the air like the infectious, slightly erotic laughter among strangers one finds in Spain. Listening in the Sheraton was an arid experience and it occurred to me that it really was like listening for the cry of the salt.

A waiter dropped a bucket of ice. No one said a word.

Over coffee I wrote down a few words: *escalator, coins, murdered kings, shoes in a corridor* . . .

I sensed that one could listen to sounds in a sequence just like Whitman did. But how could I learn Whitman's patience and live the whole day with open ears? The days turn ugly, especially in America, where public space is often filled with televisions.

Let the ugly be ugly, I thought.

Once, in London, I woke to the sound of many bicycles falling over. They were a great, artless harp. And a man's voice called out: "Bloody hell!"

Okay, I thought. *And let the ugly be part of the daylong Whitman method.*

The world is filled with spokes and gears and sudden cries.

I recalled that in the nineteenth century as musical instruments became more sophisticated there was a race to increase the pitch of orchestras. As the pitch grew higher old instruments had to be replaced or rebuilt. Technology produced the musical equivalent of the arms race.

While technology was purifying the orchestra it was also changing the soundscape. The Finnish company Nokia, which invented the cell phone, used to be a manufacturer of rubber boots. Back in the 1800s people in Finland pulled on their Nokias and sloshed through marshland to speak with their neighbors. And now the sound of boots in mud chimes electronically. Let the days be ugly.

I remembered the first time I actually heard a cell phone user.

I was waiting for a flight at LaGuardia Airport in New York.

This was around 1994 when the cell phone was first becoming affordable in the United States. I was still a Luddite as far as the cell phone was concerned: I fumbled with coins at the dirty pay phones. I thought that telephone conversations ought to take place behind closed doors.

A woman seated approximately six feet to my right began speaking without warning.

"Harry? No! I'm not going to hold this time! What? Listen! You tell that little weasel he can't have the painting! That's MY PAINTING! Look again at the prenup! No! No! No! MINE! He can have the fucking Empire sofa and the stinking carpets! He can have the locks off the doors for all I care, but that's my goddamned painting!"

Harry, whoever he was—an attorney most likely—Harry was getting the worst of it. This woman was being robbed and Harry was clearly her only line of defense. And Harry was far away. She was shouting as if the force of her voice was the medium of transmission.

"You tell that little shit that I'm going to rip his lungs out! You tell him I'm through with compromising. Tell him—tell him—WHAT? Whaddya mean you've lost his number? You expect me to sit here in LaGuardia, fat, dumb, and happy, and you want me to believe that you've lost the fucking number? Call Melman for chrissake! You call him and tell him that—"

She stopped and coughed.

"I gave away the cars, the house. I let him walk away with everything! He's not getting one thing more . . . Listening to this makes me want to puke!"

I wondered if my fellow passengers were as embarrassed by this conversation as I was. Was the woman's cell phone connected to a real person?

It was clear that the barriers between private and public conversation had collapsed and I hadn't been paying attention. I'd seen advertising for cellular calling plans on television. But after hearing this woman I would hear cell phones as if they had arrived overnight. Walking with Corky in Manhattan, I now heard the staccato one-sided conversations of businessmen who seemed to be talking to the air. One morning in a men's room in the New York Hilton I heard a man in an adjacent cubicle loudly insist to his broker that they sell his stocks. Then, without hanging up, he released his uneasy burden. Let the days be ugly.

In the machine age things were always ugly. Now the cell phone had opened public space to the tawdry business of divorce.

The woman with the cell phone boarded her flight to Cleveland. The gate area was then filled with television sounds. The Cable News Network was blasting everywhere at high volume. Men and women shouted about fashion updates, quick and easy recipes, and Hollywood gossip. There were advertisements for luxury automobiles, stock market opportunities, microwavable pizza rolls, tampons, and sugar-free chocolates.

Not long ago I woke at 3 a.m. to a television cop show and an advertisement for weight-loss tablets. A man said: "You'll never know yourself again!" I pictured Falstaff brandishing a vial of pills. I fell back asleep thinking of Falstaff the anorexic.

When I woke again there was a documentary about dancers. I heard Merce Cunningham saying something about mathematics. I wasn't awake enough to understand what he was saying. It was something about the algebraic mystery of a human body in motion, and the sublime question mark of a body standing still . . . and the heart pumping numbers through the arteries of the brain. At least this is what I now remember. Perhaps the old dancer said no such thing? I am after all an insomniac. For me, night and memory are awash in what the poet Norman Dubie calls "the greensickness of middle life."

Next I heard the composer John Cage. He was talking about the music one hears in bus stations and airports. The music of machines and happenstance, the neural, icy soundscape of a large city . . . John Cage: the maestro of spoiled environments. He said something about every sound being part of a composition.

If you really want to hear with penetration and find its associated pleasures, you must imagine you are waking up over and over again—waking on your feet, becoming aware "in medias res." The John Cage method is the Whitman method. The modernist composer wants the ugliness of both the notes and the intervals to have meaning.

I have learned in my own way how to put this system to use. You try to wake up to the quick transformations in a soundscape, especially the ugly ones.

I was visiting a tiny Finnish town one summer with my friend, the poet David Weiss. We'd gone to Orivesi to hear music by a youth orchestra. They were going to play Tchaikovsky's violin concerto with Pekka Kuusisto, one of the rising stars in the world of violinists. Before the concert David and I went to our hotel for a nap. We slept with the windows open to the summer air. We woke abruptly to the songs of a local drunkard. He was just below our window, lying flat on his back in the grass, staring up at the June sky. "Oh," he sang, mournfully, tunelessly, "oh mother, mother, I am no good! Oh, but why did you leave me!" He stopped just then because there was a squeal of brakes. This was an exquisite moment in the soundscape. I translated the drunkard's song for David. "And then his mythic mother hit the brakes," I said. She'd returned for her son after decades. We could picture the drunkard's mother leaping from her car. She would explain that she'd been asleep under a mountain, a prisoner of ancient Finnish magic.

I related to David my newfound practice. "I'm trying," I said, "to hear little compositional moments—recitatives—in the ordinary seconds when I'm not thinking at all about music. I want to wake up all day long." I admitted to him how silly this is.

"But if you're blind," I said, "you need to make hearing as pleasurable as sight-seeing.

"I suppose," I went on, "that one needs to be open all the time to lucky possibilities in the soundscape. These things might be a personal 'found music'—an approximation of the visual world."

David pointed out that visual sight-seeing is just an unending series of triggers. Object hits retina.

The object is translated instantly into analogy or metaphor.

This is the core of visual pleasure.

It is the thing we *think* we see that thrills us. The imagination is always trying to make sense of surprise.

Later as we were listening to Pekka Kuusisto's rendition of Tchaikovsky's violin concerto in a packed high school auditorium, a housefly found its way beneath my seat. My new guide dog Vidal tried to remain still. But the fly would have none of it. The fly landed on the dog's nose. It flew dizzyingly around his floppy Labrador ears. Vidal shook his head. His metal dog tags struck the legs of the chair. Pekka Kuusisto was approaching the glass church of sound that comes at the end of the Tchaikovsky concerto. Now the dog and the housefly were dueling just a few feet away from the great violinist. Poor Vidal: he was performing the fly's composition. It was the ghost of John Cage that put these creatures together. I held the dog's head between my hands, hoping to restore silence. I wondered where the fly had traveled from. Orivesi is famous for its thoroughbred horses. I thought of the fly's path from a horse barn to the concert hall. The fly left the stable about the time David and I were listening to the drunkard's song. While we walked the quiet streets and talked about seeing and hearing, the fly worked its way across Orivesi's only intersection. While Pekka Kuusisto was applying resin to his bow in a little backstage room, the fly was circling a schoolgirl's ice cream cone outside the auditorium. David and I and Vidal had come all the way from North America to hear Pekka Kuusisto in this out-of-the-way Finnish town and the fly had found its way through an open door and down a corridor. The violinist had driven from his summer house. And now the composition had come together: a cosmic instance of string theory—these vibrations were meant to happen; were always meant to happen; would happen over and over again. The dog's chain shook. The concerto rose toward its breathless conclusion.

Later, back in Helsinki, I told David I thought that listening daylong in a state of attentive waking may be more difficult than sight-seeing.

"It feels as though one has to bring joy to the soundscape—I mean, you must hold the chance sounds in place for a moment and do something with this—it's a hard thing."

We were walking on Mannerheim Street, one of Helsinki's busiest roads. Trolley cars clanged past. Someone raced by us on Rollerblades.

"If you're visual," I said, "you can scan the horizon and change your view directly. And your subconscious has a billion nearly instantaneous surprises. Listening to the world is so much slower."

I was complaining because even after a lifetime of blindness I still have vision envy.

David was carefully reading signs. We walked slowly. Vidal was heeling beside us. In some cases I translated the things David was reading. The National Opera was closed for the summer.

You have to stay open for the chance sounds, I told myself. *Make headlines for yourself if you have to:* Wind Rips Opera Banner; Men Stick Their Chins Out—Feet Walk Fast . . . Fly Orbits Pekka Kuusisto: Dog Joins Concerto; Old Women Look Disapproving in Back Row . . .

I reminded myself that the world, the ears, the imagination, all make a strange echo.

David had stopped. He was reading a sign.

"It appears," he said, "that the City Museum of Helsinki is having an exhibition of Russian underwear."

Together we read the sign in Finnish and English.

It was true. The underpants of Soviet tyranny were on display.

We'd been walking the ordinary sidewalk that borders the park, a park still fragrant with lilacs, when David had spotted a pink sign shaped like a pair of legs. The legs protruded from a pair of enormous cartoon underpants.

Beneath the bloomers there was prose explaining that the exhibition was about the human body's memories of oppression and proletarian mass production.

Of course the museum was closed for the time being.

A woman passed us and spoke in Finnish into her phone.

"Yes," she said, "go down a street, just go down a street . . ."

I resumed making headlines: *Five Year Plan Promises Fruit of Loom; Tchaikovsky Spoiled by Insect; Lilacs Stir in Baltic Wind . . .*

"Yes," said the woman with the cell phone, "simply go down the street. Nothing will bite you."

I resolved to live as much as possible like a man waking up.

Chance phrases, I thought, *sudden felicities, the ear's events come in like riderless horses.*

16. *Intersection: New York City*

———◆———

— FOR GEORGINA KLEEGE

It was March and terribly cold. I'd lost track of my location but thought I was standing near Eighth Street: that lethal sluice of traffic I'd have to cross if I wanted to go south on Fifth Avenue. This corner creates an audible anomaly: wind pours through the streets running west to east, and as it pushes through the gaps between buildings it makes white noise—the steady whisper audio engineers aim to reproduce with sound-reduction headphones. As you stand there the traffic vanishes as if by magic.

I was working my way south on Fifth and eavesdropping as I walked. Two students from New York University, both women, were talking about jazz. They had gone to the Blue Note to hear Oscar Peterson. They had grown up on Madonna but now they were grooving in New York and I was happy to be hearing about it.

Then I was standing in the strange white noise of the west-going-to-east Hudson River wind. I stood on tiptoe on the lip of the curb and thought about Oscar Peterson and how he used to accompany Ella Fitzgerald and I was thinking of Ella singing "Angel Eyes" and I told Corky to go forward. I was remembering Ella's dulcet whisper at the end of the song and Oscar Peterson's understated piano coming in for just a few bars. I said "forward" to the dog because I heard no traffic whatsoever.

What happened next was clear-cut: Corky pulled backward and I felt a rush of air across my face. Then I heard the roar of a crosstown bus. The street corner had once again masked its traffic sounds.

After my adrenaline was back to normal I walked around the block and reapproached the same corner. The wind was astonishing both in its force and in its absolute efficiency at blocking the sounds of cars and buses. I stood for a few minutes on the east side of Fifth Avenue on the north side of Eighth Street and listened with what I can only call reverence. I thought of Igor Stravinsky, who insisted that most people, including composers, often fail to listen with effort. Stravinsky wanted us to hear beyond the narrow coil of easy expectations.

So I stood for a while and I learned that the wind in that place has three distinct auditory characteristics.

The big wind kills traffic. The whole world sounds like flags in a hurricane. The wind rips through spaces between brownstones and that wind is surely a god, as the Greeks well knew.

Under the big wind is a funny effect—one might call it the durational absentmindedness of wind—for whole moments the wind doesn't exactly stop, but it shifts direction, and you can hear everything in the city with absolute clarity. Along with the trucks you hear the bicycle deliverymen—you hear the chains of their bikes and the gritty noise of gears. There's a clatter of a loose manhole cover as a bus hits it. You notice a woman laughing on the far side of Fifth Avenue—she is a mezzo-soprano, loud and high and laughing to beat the band. And then she's gone.

The last trick of the wind is the cleverest of all. Wind can transmit sounds or echoes if it wants to. Between the white noise and my own pulse I can hear electric lines and something metallic clattering and something that sounds like an oboe and of course I'll never know what this is. Nevertheless the wind carries fragments of noise from far places like an absentminded uncle who doesn't remember what's in his old suitcase.

I stood in that place where just fifteen minutes earlier I had almost been killed. When the wind paused I could feel the sun on my face and hear the radio from a taxicab. Then the traffic was swallowed once more. The wind was back with news of its spacious, inverted, colorless landscape.

17. Airports

———◆———

There was a waterfall in the hotel's lobby and then there was a woman's voice which was also soft and I had to lean in close to hear her words. She was offering gently to cure me. I'd stopped by the rushing water to get my bearings. I was searching for the exit so I could take my dog outside. I knew I had to turn right at the waterfall. And now here she was, the waterfall woman, inviting me to join her church and be healed.

Her congregation, she said, had recently cured two blind people: a boy and an old woman. Both had been sightless but through the power of Christ they had been restored. Just behind the waterfall I could hear a Muzak rendition of "Hey Jude." Somewhere nearby a stepladder creaked as a worker changed lightbulbs. I couldn't think of a thing to say. I thought of salmon returning to their spawning pools, fish battering against the stones.

The woman pressed on. She said she had recently been named "Catholic Woman of the Year" somewhere in Ohio. She spoke with ardor about faith and healing and the laying on of hands.

The stepladder man closed his aluminum ladder with a satisfying snap and moved away. I listened to him go with a series of squeaks. Finally I said I had already been healed. Then I said that I urgently needed to take my dog outside. I raced off in the general direction of the door.

These spiritual infringements happen all the time. I'm always standing still at the edge of a hotel lobby or in a parking lot when the moment occurs. Once in a diner on the New Jersey Turnpike I was alone at a table while my friend was getting coffee. I was listening to the delicate voices of children at a nearby table. They were admiring my dog. They were asking their father how the dog knows what I'm thinking. They thought that a dog guide was psychic. I was enjoying this idea when I felt a tap on my shoulder. Again it was a woman's voice. "I would like very much," she said, "to pray for you if you'd let me." The kids at the near table were laughing because their father was making bubbles with his drinking straw. Life was unfolding splendidly at their little table. "Listen," I said, "I really don't require prayers." I stopped for a moment. I needed to hold myself back. I didn't want to plunge headlong into a theological debate. I didn't want to say that my permission might not be required for authentic prayer. The children's laughter was very sweet. "Listen," I said with a smile I hoped would seem avuncular, "I have a happy life and at just this moment I don't require any prayers." She said nothing in return and merely walked away. When my friend Richard came back I imagined her watching us as we crossed the parking lot. I wondered if maybe she was praying for me anyway. I imagined her walking her daily rounds and searching for prayerful opportunities. I pictured her scanning each room for a person with a disability. She must think that disabled people are lonely and lost.

Some of the strangers I meet suspect that I can't hear. Perhaps the suspicion that blind people are deaf has something to do with the popularity of *The Miracle Worker*—the film about the life of Helen Keller starring Patty Duke.

Not long ago while I was waiting for a plane in Chicago's O'Hare Airport a woman talked about me as if I didn't exist— cooing about the guide dog: "What a beautiful dog, look at his eyes! So expressive! Look at those adorable ears!" And then she was off and running, telling her companion, who never got a word in, that it must be very difficult to go places "like that" and then she talked about me in the third person. I pictured her using her hands extravagantly. "He's brave to be traveling alone like that. I wonder if he has someone with him." I couldn't stand it anymore. I picked up my rucksack and called the dog and we left. We had an hour to kill before our next flight. Time for coffee . . . Time for body waxing . . . Oh anything rather than listen to this woman's description of my life . . .

Blindness is a traveling exhibit.

At the airport Starbucks I'm greeted with silence from the cashier. I'm smiling. I'm looking in what I imagine is the proper direction. I'm wearing dark glasses. I have a dog with a harness. I say hello. Ask if it's my turn. And there's more silence. I hear spoons tinkling and someplace behind me a public-address announcement alerts passengers of a gate change for the flight to Milwaukee.

The cashier must think that blind men don't travel alone or don't drink coffee. Or don't have money. Or we are loose from the asylum without the white-coated attendant and the cashier probably wonders why they don't have a panic button behind the counter as they do in most banks. Blind customer . . . Tap toe on button. Call for attendants.

A customer behind me is impatient. "The man wants to buy some coffee," he says to the cashier.

Cashier: "You want coffee?"

"Yes, coffee. Black. Shaken, not stirred."

More silence.

"What kind of coffee?" The question is clearly unfriendly.

The line behind me has grown long. I imagine that it stretches back into ancient Mesopotamia.

"What kinds of coffee do you have?" I ask the question and keep my smile. It's an American smile. Dale Carnegie . . . A smile that widens if it finds a small measure of civilization.

So of course I get the house blend and I get a plastic lid for the top which requires the cashier to actually walk five feet to the place where the plastic lids are prominently displayed for the normal customers. He does this because pointing and mumbling "over there" can't answer my question about how to acquire a protective top. I smile. And I smile as I walk aimlessly looking for a seat where I can drink the coffee.

So there I was: the golem with coffee. Frankenstein in weighted shoes. I was in a seating area and hundreds of people were talking like jackhammers. I stood still and shifted the blistering coffee from hand to hand. A businessman barked into his cell phone about "the meeting" with Riley. "Yeah, I missed the meeting with Riley. Fucking United canceled the flight. Tell Riley I'm in O'Hare and the next flight doesn't leave until five-thirty. No. Don't give him the pictures. I need to make the pitch. Pitch. Then pictures. Just wait for me." Then there was the snap of his cell phone as he shut it without saying goodbye.

A woman who must have been sitting at the cell phone man's table said, "Clarissa's soaked." And Clarissa, who must have been around two years old, said, "I'm not soaked!" And I had the sense that the cell phone man was looking me up and down. I always feel it. When the sighted look you over it feels like you've walked into a ghost in the woods. The cell phone man was examining me. My hand felt like it was blistering from the coffee and then my dog pulled backward. Someone at a nearby table was calling him. I had to fight to keep my balance and hold the coffee.

A strong hand grabbed me around my left arm. My left arm was hanging on to the dog. A woman's voice was telling the dog that her own dog also likes popcorn. The hand that held me had a voice. It was a man's voice. It said, "Here, come over here. There's a seat here." Coffee was running down my right wrist. I was now moving my feet, being led by a stranger, trying to keep my balance, aiming to look professional, hoping to make it look easy. Then we were at a table and my mystery guide let go of me and disappeared.

A taped announcement urged passengers to be conscious of terrorism.

A woman's bracelets tinkled.

I thought of how those bracelets were the sound of freedom. The braceleted woman could go anywhere.

I felt as though I was sitting in a construction of clay and soot. When I got up to move, all eyes would be on me. I would have to walk the stage of the ordinary gate area. I would appear as weird as a man carrying an ivory bowl.

I thought I was returning to my departure gate but instead I was in a new corridor. I stepped on something that felt like an iron grate. It was a moving walkway and suddenly I was sailing through the terminal in the wrong direction. I heard mariachi music from a shop. A man's laughter . . . The man laughed like a baying hunting dog. I heard the sound of a blender. A child cried out at the sight of my dog. I was sailing along the edge of a ruined map. I was no longer certain where I was, but I was moving quickly like one of those clowns compelled to run by a larger clown pushing a broom. And voices bellowed out the rote words of the airport—"Don't leave bags unattended"; "Electric car to

United Gate 33B"; "The flight to Des Moines is now loaded and the gate has been closed."

And then I was falling forward because I'd hit the end of the belt without warning and my dog was clattering ahead of me. His toenails made a sound like dropped marbles... I let go of his leash and fell to my knees and lost my backpack in the process. Why wasn't there some kind of warning, some kind of taped announcement at the end of the walkway? I was on my knees and reaching for my backpack or the dog, whichever I could find first, when a woman handed me the dropped bag. She had a Brooklyn accent. She asked if we were okay. I asked her if she could see the dog's feet. I was worried he might have lost a nail at the end of the beltway. I pictured his bleeding paw. But he was fine. We were both fine. I was back on my feet. Vidal was wagging his tail.

The Brooklyn woman wanted to know if we needed help.

Before I could answer I heard an astonishing sound. It was a sound like a very heavy bowling ball rolling down an alley. A bowling ball with a ticking clock inside. What in the hell could it be?

It turned out to be a defective wheelchair which was being pushed by a man who worked for one of the airlines. He stopped. After a moment he said, "You want a ride?"

The Brooklyn woman was indignant, and said with sudden vehemence that I was blind and not lame.

The man with the wheelchair was unconcerned.

"Maybe the dog would like a ride?" he said.

His accent sounded vaguely foreign but I couldn't place it.

I asked him if he could escort us to our gate.

He was cheerful about this and told me to follow him. I thanked the Brooklyn woman and set out behind the man with the chair. It was easy to follow him, the chair resumed the bowling-ball noise.

We walked this way for a long time. The wheelchair man went ahead with his conquering apparatus and Vidal and I trailed along by ear. I was starting to wonder how far I had gone on the mechanical beltway since we had been walking for what seemed like fifteen minutes. Then the chair man stopped.

"We will take the elevator," he said.

I didn't reply but wondered why we needed to take the elevator since I hadn't changed floors after leaving my original gate. We descended in silence. I figured my escort must know the ropes. The doors slid open and again the chair went forward with its tremendous racket.

As I followed I sensed that we were now in an underground corridor. We were no longer navigating in commercial space and had entered a kind of steam tunnel.

I was aware of my innocence.

I was depending on this man and the sound of his broken wheelchair to lead me through a tunnel.

Soon we were at another elevator.

"This way we get past security," said Chair Man.

I didn't know what he was talking about. I shouldn't need to go through security a second time. We were merely going to my gate. I said something to that effect. The elevator arrived.

"You need to go through security but it's a big fuss," he said. "I'll get you through by going a different way."

I got on the elevator. We rode for about twenty-five seconds and entered a new corridor. The wheelchair growled in protest as we started forward.

"The disability people have trouble with the security." The chair man was beginning to talk.

"I'm going to get you past them."

Then we were going down in another elevator.

We were again in a basement.

"Do you believe in Jesus?" The chair man was suddenly interested in my spiritual life.

"Yes," I said. The chair man had stopped pushing the chair.

"Jesus cured the blind." The chair man said this as though I might not have known. Then he didn't say anything at all. We stood in the strange corridor and someone passed us with something large that was rolling on castors. I had this momentary picture in my mind of an airport worker pushing a huge rolling Jesus figurine. Then the sound of Jesus wheels vanished and we were alone again.

"Listen," I said. "Jesus sits beside the road and our job is to walk the road and follow his instructions. That's all I have to say on the subject. Let's get going before I miss my flight."

I could smell whiskey and knew that the chair man was drunk.

"All right," he said, "all right you know Jesus is still loving you."

We went through some metal doors and much to the chair man's dismay we were in the security area. After all that walking and plotting he had made an enormous circle.

When I finally got on my plane and settled Vidal under my feet I wondered about the miles that humanity walks uphill in search of a cure. It's strange enough to be a symbol for other people's curative longings, but it's odder still to be the figure of spiritual transference—as though in receiving Jesus the disabled verify the faith of disheartened Christians. My blindness represents a promise of rescue to others. I was mulling this over when I became aware that the man next to me was staring without saying hello. There was a vacant seat between us. He didn't think I knew he was examining me. But he was definitely looking my way and Vidal, sensing this, put his head up on the empty seat. The dog's move would start the conversation.

"If you don't mind my asking," said the stranger, "how did you go blind?"

"I was born this way," I said, and tried to calculate how many times I'd been asked this question. I thought of how it might work in reverse, if I were to say, "How did you become such a nondescript little nebbish in a cheap business suit?" But of course I did no such thing. It's easier to get out of the intrusive moment if you can remain monosyllabic.

"Oh, born that way?" he said then, as if he were remarking about the ingredients in a French stew. "Oh, ground goose livers in the cassoulet? How unexpected!"

"Were your parents blind?"

"No," I said, "not at first, but now they are."

"Glaucoma?" asked the stranger.

"No: death," I said. "My parents are dead. As the ancient Greeks well knew, all dead people are blind."

"Oh," he said, "you are a philosopher?"

I saw this wasn't going well. I'd violated my monosyllable rule with a joke about dead people. I wondered what other mistakes I could now make. I could for instance tell him I was a writer. That would be a monumental blunder. The poet W. H. Auden once remarked that the best way he knew to end airplane conversation was to tell people he was a medieval historian.

"Yes," I said, "I am a philosopher."

"Really?" he said, as if he had discovered Spanish sausage in the cassoulet.

"And what do you do?" I figured I should push a pawn.

"By day," he said, pausing for effect, "I work for the airline as a systems analyst." Then he paused again. He was going to talk about Richard Rorty and postanalytic philosophy—I could feel it coming.

"But in my own time," he said, pausing again, "in my own time I am a firewalker!"

"Ah," I said, "I'll bet you can't do that in the airport!"

He leaned close to me then. His breath was heavy with the scent of garlic.

"Have you ever read the books of Carlos Casteneda?"

I wanted to stand up, make my way into the aisle, and kick myself for having given this guy room to clatter around in. I was now about to enter the occult landscape of peyote and volcanoes. I remembered a college classmate circa 1973 who once insisted that he could get through college by reading only the works of Carlos Casteneda and smoking hash every day. Carlos Casteneda: guru of the Grateful Dead; shamanic traveler who visited world after world beyond the scope of the human retina. *God, I thought, how regrettable that I have made this airplane moment possible.*

"Yes I have read Carlos Casteneda," I said, "though not since the Nixon administration."

The stranger who was now "my" stranger looked at me fixedly—or so I presumed since he wasn't moving and I could smell his breath. "What do you know about fear?" he asked.

I knew it didn't matter what I said. Firewalker had found his stride.

"Fear is all around us," he said. "Fear is in the air, you have it in your bloodstream."

I nodded.

"Fear is what causes illness. All the major studies agree that fear, which the medical community likes to call 'stress,' is the cause of illness."

"Yes," I said. It occurred to me that I'd never heard of a single reputable study naming stress as the direct cause of disease, but this wasn't going to be a reality-based discussion.

"I can bring you to my ranch where together we conquer fear.

"Fear is all around you," he said then. "You are afraid. And I can help you."

I nodded again.

"I've cured people with multiple sclerosis," he said. "They put aside their fear and walk through fire.

"I've cured people of mental diseases like schizophrenia.

"We walk twelve feet over the live coals and then fear is gone and once fear is gone we enter a new world without pain."

"I'm not in pain," I said then, and was pleased to notice how convincing my voice sounded. "I'm not in pain and my blindness isn't remotely connected with fear or abjection or petit mal or cosmic suffering."

"Oh you can say that but wait until you have walked through the flames," he said.

I knew better than to continue. I wasn't going to argue about the true facts associated with walking over coals. I knew that once wood is sufficiently burned it acts as an insulator—that people can walk quickly over hot charcoal without feeling a thing. I'd read this in a magazine called *The Skeptical Inquirer* published by a group of scientists who travel the world debunking claims by occultists. I sank lower into my seat and said I had to sleep.

"You don't know what you're missing," said Firewalker. I was quiet, leaning on the pillow I'd tucked against the far corner of my seat.

When I got back home to Columbus, Ohio, my wife read aloud a short article from a suburban weekly newspaper. The woman from the Holiday Inn who had offered to cure me as we stood beside the lobby waterfall had been named Catholic

Woman of the Year. The newspaper suggested without irony that she had cured people with disabilities in her congregation. My wife stopped reading and suggested helpfully that I forget about blindness and let this ministry cure the tendonitis in my right shoulder.

I thought of how three strangers had offered to cure me over the past forty-eight hours and then I remembered these lines by the poet Marvin Bell:

It's life that is hard: waking, sleeping, eating, loving, working / and dying are easy.

I knew then that I needed to wear Marvin's poem on a shirt whenever I'm knocking around in the public dark.

18. The Tenor of Ocean City, Brooklyn

———◆———

It was the Ides of March and New York was rising toward spring like most northeastern coastal cities: there was a cold breeze and soon a big wind swept over the streets. Old neighborhoods smelled like the ocean again. In Ocean City someone had placed a white camellia in a bedroom window. The window was dirty but it didn't matter: this was the season of fresh detail.

I received these particulars secondhand. All my friends eventually become play-by-play radio announcers.

Ocean City was not Manhattan. It didn't even feel like Brooklyn. James described polite suburban houses from the 1940s postwar boom: the two- and three-story houses faced each other on narrow streets. The houses had wide front porches and flagstone walks and some had white picket fences that enclosed shrines to the Blessed Virgin.

James and I had come to Brooklyn because we were opera enthusiasts and we had heard that Ocean City is home to the Enrico Caruso Museum of America. We had hired a car service to bring us here. Our driver Joe was from the Bronx but he knew the neighborhood because he was into real estate. "These houses are worth a fortune," he said. I wondered why the Caruso museum was all the way out here and guessed that the museum was a family venture.

All we knew about the museum was that it was located at 1942 East 19th Street and it was open to the public by appointment only and the director was a man named Aldo Mancusi.

I'd written to Signore Mancusi by electronic mail telling him that I was a midwestern professor who was writing a book that included an appreciation of Caruso. Sitting in the backseat of the Lincoln town car I had the nagging feeling that something was missing beyond the business of identity. I suspected this had to do with my blindness—I wondered if I should have told Signore Mancusi that I had a dog guide? Visiting Italy a few years back I'd discovered that dogs for the blind weren't understood by doormen. On more than a few occasions I'd been prohibited from visiting museums by overbearing gatekeepers. Barred from entering a church grotto in Milan, I'd stood on the sidewalk and wept in the midday sun. Now I feared that Signore Mancusi would refuse me entrance to what I imagined must be his home. I expected that he lived alone with the Great Caruso's ghost.

I had time to fret because we'd gotten lost. Joe drove patiently through the quiet streets of Ocean City. The Lincoln moved through the empty neighborhoods. I thought about Caruso's ghost. If ever there was a noble, happy phantom, it would have to be the great tenor's spirit. I thought of Caruso flitting through heavily furnished rooms. He would come sideways, crablike as "O sole mio" poured from the bell of a Victrola. He would arrive for wind chimes or the cheerful noise of dropped spoons.

Caruso.

His specter accompanies Pavarotti and Plácido Domingo. It is a warming spirit. In life he was the world's first superstar. By the time of his death in 1921 Caruso's name was magic on every continent.

I remembered hearing Pavarotti say in a television interview that one could think of all the Italian tenors taken together as forming a kind of skyscraper. And Caruso, he said, was the voice that held up the building.

I wondered as he said this if he meant to suggest that his own voice was the penthouse and Caruso's was the cellar.

But Caruso's ghost would like the cellar, I thought. *In life the singer took care of an extended family of relatives and friends. He was a Neapolitan peasant who became a nobleman prince.*

Caruso. Who bought thousands of tickets to the Metropolitan Opera for New York's firemen and cops.

Who sang for presidents and kings.

Caruso would have a contented spirit.

Joe had found the house. There was a small sign in the window.

And then we were on the front porch, two men and a dog looking for the secret opera lover's pergola.

Aldo Mancusi opened the door. There was a tinkling of shop bells. He was quick to speak. His tone was soft. It was the voice of a man who is used to handling delicate objects. My heart was beating fast. "Welcome, welcome," he said, his voice smooth as a bird tamer's, "welcome to the Enrico Caruso Museum of America. Watch the stairs—will you have trouble with the stairs? We must go up." And we went up into a place that was at once a man's home and a reliquary.

"Turn left, turn left at the top of the stairs! Now you are in the main room of the museum," he said. "On the walls around us are a thousand drawings done by the Great Caruso himself. As

97

you know, the tenor used to draw cartoons for relaxation. Some of these he would give to friends, some he kept for himself. I have many cartoons as well as thousands of Caruso's letters to his famous admirers. Over there is a letter from the conductor Toscanini to Caruso. In this letter he writes of his sadness because he felt he was in a loveless marriage. In another letter over here Puccini expresses his envy of Caruso. Caruso had a way with women. As you know, the tenor always gets the girl."

Aldo Mancusi was talking fast because my blindness was an additional ghost in the room.

He was probably worried that his collection was mostly a visual display.

I was thinking that I like these moments when there are at least two ghosts in a room. Aldo Mancusi was talking with a gentle earnestness. He was a collector and he was a guardian.

The floor creaked. I heard a cough from an adjacent room. It was probably Mrs. Mancusi.

"Wow," said James, who could discern that every inch of wall space was covered with mementos. "What's this impressive medal?" He had spotted a sizable honorary badge. "That was presented to Caruso by the mayor of New York in appreciation for the tenor's service to New York City. As you know, Caruso was a beloved figure on both sides of the Atlantic. He took care of people wherever he went. He wasn't one of these artists like you see today who believe they're better than their neighbors. Caruso thought of himself as a lucky man. How many great artists today think they owe anything to luck?"

Before I had a chance to answer the question Signore Mancusi told me to put out my hand. "This is one of Caruso's shoes," he said, and placed a small and surprisingly weighty shoe in my right hand. "This is really one of Caruso's shoes," he said. "You can feel how well made it is. It's a saddle shoe with white and black leather. Caruso loved decorative shoes. This shoe is very heavy because as you know Caruso was short and he had lifts built into the heels. He was a very tiny man. He was probably no more than five feet two inches tall."

He paused for a second.

"I don't have many things for you to touch," he said. "Everything is under glass. I thought you might like to hold the tenor's shoe."

I explored the shoe with my fingers.

"His shoes were top quality," said Signore Mancusi. "Caruso had the best Italian shoemaker in New York. All his shoes were custom made. Of course the white patina of the leather has grayed a bit. When the shoes were new they were white." I fingered the laces and imagined that Caruso probably never tied his own shoes. His valet was a deeply loyal servant from Naples named Martino. I wondered when it was that Martino last shoehorned these babies onto the tenor's miniature feet. Caruso was a dandy. I pictured him wearing a canary yellow waistcoat and baggy cream-colored pants. These shoes would have come last. The tenor would have been headed for Del Pezzo's—his favorite New York restaurant. And because I was thrilled to be holding the tenor's shoe I felt the bonhomie that develops between men who are enthusiasts. I wanted to tell Signore Mancusi about Caruso's waistcoat and Martino and the little onyx shoehorn I suspected Martino must have used in 1919 when these shoes were last worn. But I didn't have time. Signore Mancusi was compelling our attention. This was his house and he had much to show us. He hurried from the shoes to a tiny framed glass box on the wall. "This," he said, "this was Caruso's last pack of cigarettes. I can't let you touch them of course. But this pack of cigarettes was in the tenor's pocket when he died. There is also in this box Caruso's ivory cigarette holder."

The display was like one of Joseph Cornell's surreal creations. There was a cigarette suspended in the center of the box. Beneath it, like a dark guppy, sat the cigarette holder.

"Caruso died young and cigarettes contributed to his death," said Signore Mancusi. He said it as though praising the softness of a gentleman's hands.

"These were Egyptian cigarettes. Caruso smoked three packs a day. Can you imagine a singer doing that today?"

I marveled that Signore Mancusi had obtained Caruso's last cigarette. When the singer died in Naples there must have been a coterie of scavengers hanging around the tenor's hotel. I pictured the dead man's small effects, cigarettes and shoes being passed quickly from hand to hand between elevator operators and bellboys until the things were safely hidden in the streets.

"Here," said Signore Mancusi, "here is a life mask of Caruso's face. There are only two of these in the world. You can touch it."

I felt the plaster curve of the forehead and the sockets of the eyes. Once, on a tour of the Perkins School for the Blind in Watertown, I was invited to put my hands on a plaster copy of Laura Bridgeman's brain. Ms. Bridgeman was the first blind-deaf student to master the arts of reading and writing, at least in America. I hated touching these things.

"Caruso had such a regal face," I said.

"Yes," said Signore Mancusi. "He was a very handsome man."

I handed the mask back and we moved quickly to a new display, a rebuilt Victrola of sorts. In fact, it was the world's first electrically operated jukebox. It was built in the early twenties by the Mills Novelty Company, which also made gambling machines. This particular jukebox was installed in a New York City barroom just after the tenor's death.

The thing was as large as a player piano. It had a wooden cabinet with small windows that allowed the listener to see the record being played. When it started it made elusive mechanical sounds. It reminded me of a printing press. There was a noise of springs and armatures and rotating drums. Finally there was the hiss of a gramophone needle as it entered the grooves of a disk. And for a split second we heard Caruso's voice and then something happened, there was a flaw in the old mechanism, the record slowed and the great voice descended sickeningly into a moan.

"Oh dear," said Aldo Mancusi, "this shouldn't happen. Let me unplug the machine and then plug it in again. Sometimes that restores things. It gets out of kilter."

Again there was a sound of hidden instruments arranging themselves. Then the needle hit the record. Caruso's voice stirred from the speaker. The voice was big. Even on primitive recordings it has always sounded like a voice that could part clouds. But again the music ground to a halt in a sad manner. The voice darkened and slowed, then vanished into the belly of silence.

"I must take this machine apart," said Signore Mancusi. "It needs to have the belts realigned. But back in its glory days people put money right here into this and they could hear the great tenor whenever they wanted."

He wound up another Victrola with a lacquered black horn that resembled an umbrella blown backward by wind. Again there was the crackling of the needle as it pressed into the grooves. The song was "Torna a Surriento." For a moment we heard only the poorly recorded and tinny mandolins and then Caruso's voice poured from the quivering trumpet. Hearing this sound in Aldo Mancusi's living room, I felt myself being stretched and narrowed at the same time. Sadness put its hands on my chest. The hiss of the Victrola squeezed me somehow. For over a hundred years Caruso's voice has sustained lonesome people everywhere. I wondered if Signore Mancusi ever experienced this sadness. I realized that I couldn't ask him, that the question would be indecorous.

Once upon a time as a boy in New Orleans Louis Armstrong learned how to sing by listening to his mother's Caruso records. Eighty years ago this was the most famous voice in the world. Forty years ago in my childhood it was a voice in the attic. Nowadays, despite Caruso's legendary place among tenors or his unchallenged standing in musical history, his voice has been reduced by the medium that recorded it. Loving this weakly recorded sound is a distressed activity, like loving the countryside in late November. Fans of Caruso long to be taken to a pure location just above the earth where, just for once, we might hear the great singer as Puccini heard him. After Puccini listened to Caruso for the first time, he is reported to have said, "Who sent you to me? God?"

We walked from the living room to an adjoining den where visitors to the museum can watch a silent film featuring the tenor. Caruso appeared in a 1918 film entitled *My Cousin*. He played two Italian immigrant brothers in New York: one was a starving sculptor and the other was a famous opera star. The film showed Little Italy and the stage of the old Metropolitan Opera House. Despite the lack of sound, critics praised the extraordinary mobility of Caruso's astonishing face. But standing before the movie posters of the day, I have the feeling that Caruso is vanishing before me like a man seen through the wrong end of a telescope. I can only hear his recorded voice in memory singing "E lucevan le stelle." Perhaps sensing my mood, Aldo Mancusi said: "We will not stay in this room. There's nothing here for you. Caruso died just before the invention of the talking films. It is too bad. It is really too bad."

We moved to the rear of the house. Signore Mancusi wanted me to hear and touch things. I felt as if I'd returned to my grandmother's attic. We walked through a labyrinth of rooms and passageways and then we stopped abruptly in front of an artifact that Aldo Mancusi said was unrelated to Caruso. "I was able to acquire this a few years back," he said, "and you can touch it. It's some of the original cable from Roebling's Brooklyn Bridge." I reached out and grasped the steel. It was hanging from a spool. "This original cable was defective and Roebling had to replace miles of it. Now feel this," he said, and I put my hand on a metal plate that had been perforated with tiny holes. "That's a precursor to the audio record. It went inside this hand-cranked organ." He slipped the disk into a mahogany box and drew my hand to a wooden crank on the side. "Go ahead and turn it," he said. "You can hear what the world sounded like before Caruso."

Aldo Mancusi was guiding me toward an audio epiphany. The machine, the Gem hand organ, was popular in American living rooms in the last decade of the nineteenth century. While Caruso's recordings may be unappealing by today's standards, the sound of this parlor instrument was joyless. When I turned the crank, notes flared like struck matches as air pushed through the holes in the metal dish. Someone once thought these notes were sweet. But the sound was heartless and unremitting. I imagined an upper-class woman of Brooklyn Heights turning this handle as Roebling's dynamite detonated in the distance.

I tried to work out some historical arithmetic. The invention of the talking machine changed how we listen and amplified a new type of leisure-class distraction. By 1902 people could listen to Caruso on afternoons when they were desperate for all the usual reasons; one could set a record spinning and hear the "Lamento di Federico" from Cilea's *L'Arlesiana*. Suddenly people could buy some belief in the operations of the soul. How extraordinary that the first artist to prove that recorded music was possible was also quite likely the greatest tenor of them all.

Aldo Mancusi showed us some other hand organs but now I was lost in thought. I pictured the poet Hart Crane in 1919 writing his poem "The Bridge" while he listened repeatedly to his Victrola. Crane often thought he might jump from the Brooklyn Bridge. I wondered how many people during the past hundred years had been spared, at least for a time, by nothing more than the phonograph?

I'd come to Ocean City thinking that I'd find some ironic urban story or a ghost. But Signore Mancusi's collection showed me how recorded music and Caruso's voice called millions into the parlors of the middle classes. All at once there was a place for the richness of the world in common houses.

On the way back to Manhattan James and I shared our perspectives. There was something palpable in the Caruso museum, something about the value of loss. We had seen the tenor's coin collection. I'd held the man's shoe up to my ear like a seashell.

We both recognized that we'd been moved by the passion of Aldo Mancusi. In a funny way I think we felt like boys riding bicycles. Listening to vintage opera records makes one feel alive and a bit lonely in the world's weather.

19. Blue Lagoon

———◆———

It was an improbable package tour. We'd come to Iceland for no better reason than to hear Cuban music. We were three men visiting Reykjavík to hear the Buena Vista Social Club and smoke cigars.

Gary was driving our rented Ford Escort and describing what he saw. His friend Greg, a weight lifter, was riding shotgun. The man could barely move.

"Look over there," said Gary. "There's a pile of volcanic rocks that looks like the Michelin Man!"

"I can't turn my head," said Greg. "My seat belt is around my throat."

"Are there any birds?" I asked from the backseat. I was held in position by suitcases.

"Every living creature appears to have been eaten." Gary said. "Wait," he added, "there are some algae on the rocks off to the right."

I remembered that Giacomo Puccini was reputed to have eaten all the ducks in Italy. "Maybe Puccini was once in Iceland," I said.

This was no more improbable than the appearance in Iceland of the Buena Vista Social Club—a group of veteran Havana nightclub performers who had returned to the stage after a long hiatus enforced by Fidel Castro. They'd won a Grammy. They had a movie. They were on a world tour. The average age of the group's musicians was just over eighty.

It was April and very cold. The northern sky was brighter and bluer than we'd imagined. Though Reykjavík is a relatively small city, we managed to get lost. We drove in tight and hopeless circles down streets that were all named in honor of Snorri Sturluson, the Icelandic epic poet. It felt reassuring to be lost in a town where everything was named for a poet. Being lost on a poet's street is different than, say, being lost on I-80.

"We've just turned off Snorri Street and we're back on Snorri Street," said Gary. "We will soon be in Greenland."

It was Gary who had first seen the advertisement for a Cuban getaway in Iceland. He called me while I was preparing to teach a class.

"Icelandic Air has a deal," he said. "We can hear hot Cuban music in Reykjavík. Fly round-trip from New York. Get concert tickets, air tickets, and three hotel nights, all for five hundred dollars. Hell, it's a perfect sound-montage escape."

"All right," I said. I thought: *Why not go to Iceland where the only sounds are from the volcanic fissures between the rocks; where the North Atlantic wind rips over the stones; where people whisper in the restaurants and there is a musical chiming of shrimp forks on the fine china.*

And then there was the promise of postmodernity, all that long-suppressed Cuban dance floor music amplified in the Icelandic night. How perfect. And cheap. It was easy to say yes.

So here I was, officially sight-seeing by ear in a very cold place. After we found our hotel and checked in I switched on the radio and caught a few moments of Bach's "Goldberg Variations" as played by Glenn Gould.

There were no sounds coming from the adjacent rooms. No scrape of furniture. No clearing of an old man's throat. The room was frigid and silent and Glenn Gould's essential loneliness expanded in slow waves. The music was like a lake at night. I massaged my temples and leaned back into a pillow. There was something both delicate and ponderous about the music. It produced in me that delirium in which you don't know whether to laugh or cry. I fell asleep.

When I woke up Gary had arrived to suggest we go to a nearby hot springs. He had already been jogging the length of Reykjavík's harbor and he had located the civic baths. We walked with Greg in a bone-chilling wind through slate gray light, our teeth chattering. I could still hear Bach in the fibrous places beneath my face. Then there was a synchronized click of small locks. We were putting away our clothing in a tidy municipal locker room. The Icelanders in the men's locker room talked together like men in a boat. Their voices were low. Their words soft. Small boys spoke to their fathers. The men's voices were shade. The little boy's voices were circles of light. It was Sunday. Early spring. The sun was growing stronger on the North Sea.

The baths were meticulously designed. I'd imagined a kind of natural grotto but instead the city had constructed pools fed by geothermal springs. Every pool had underwater benches in man-made nooks. I could hear that people were emerging from the winter and steaming away the ache of hibernation. I relied on Gary and Greg for my descriptions. I saw smoke and aqua distillations of sky and water. The people were orchid-colored fog. I leaned back and felt the essential gratitude of my bones. I thought of my bones as dry twigs and imagined the mineral balm of the Icelandic water was working its way gently into my marrow. It was, I thought, fair wondrous to be alive. And the air above the pool was so cold and fresh. I pulled my head below the surface and then rose up into the chill atmosphere.

A church bell tolled across the harbor. Gulls called as they circled. A little girl laughed at something her mother said in the universal song of a nursery rhyme.

Gary and Greg had discovered that there were other pools surrounding us, each heated to a unique temperature. It turned out you could increase your steaming pleasure. I'd been floating in the kiddie pool.

Gary offered me his elbow and we crossed icy stones to the next circle of bathing bliss. We plunged into an opening in the ground that sounded like a steam kettle.

I heard a strange whistle from my larynx. There were five of us in this grotto, all men, all groaning and holding on to the edges of the pool. We could not speak. We were merely vessels of escaping breath. Our throats were open. We made visceral and unintentional songs of exhalation. I heard the sound of glass marbles rolling inside my skull.

Walking back to the hotel through the harbor, we studied the architectural landmarks. "I think that's the place where the Buena Vistas are singing," said Greg. Gary and Greg had learned the shorthand that goes with blind walking. "Curb up," said Greg. "Curb down." "Five steps up." I was walking without my guide dog—dogs from overseas are forbidden in Iceland owing to agricultural quarantine laws. I tapped with my cane and my friends tried to alert me when something orthopedic was about to happen. "Jeez," said Gary, "don't take this the wrong way, but being blind must be a pain in the ass." "Only when you fall down," I said. I heard a heavy crane somewhere off to my right. I imagined it was unloading Energizer batteries and toothpicks. Hardly anything is manufactured in Iceland. There are almost no trees. Toothpicks must be a big import item. Toothpicks from Minnesota that are shrink-wrapped in China. The crane was squeaking rhythmically as though it was sending Morse code. I liked this notion and thought of the crane ditting Morse code poetry while depositing industrial pallets of Sterno and enormous boxes of false teeth. Squeaking cables were releasing Snorri Sturluson's poetry into the frigid ocean air.

We had come to Iceland to hear Cuban musicians whose work had been forgotten in Havana for more than forty years. The Cuban nightclubs went silent after Castro's revolution. A profound Latin jazz tradition was driven into back rooms. North Americans knew only Desi Arnaz, whose TV character Ricky Ricardo played Cuban rumba at the Tropicana. I remembered there was an episode of *I Love Lucy* in which Lucille Ball disguised herself in a Carmen Miranda getup complete with a fruit basket headdress so as to appear onstage against her husband's wishes. But maybe I was remembering this wrong. I could go to the Museum of Television and Radio in New York and find out. While real Cuban musicians were forced offstage, Lucille Ball was vamping in New York.

The Icelandic people were indisputably lit up about the appearance of the Buena Vista Social Club. The living heat of Havana's jazz had awakened something palpable here in the North Sea. I'd always liked thinking about the human life-force, the invisible chi that ignites when music arrives and the local air is changed. The Beatles' arrival in Manhattan in 1964 sparked something because the Mersey beat was essentially a needed awakening. This had happened before in New York. Sixty years earlier Caruso arrived at the Metropolitan Opera and rich and poor alike flocked to hear the tenor. The singer was so beloved by New Yorkers that when he was ill the police put hay in the street to dull the clatter of trolleys and horses' hooves.

The night wind was amazingly cold, as if some god of the northern sea had been affronted by spring. I heard a blues line in my head: "There's winds out on the ocean / Just blowin' where they choose / But them winds ain't got no emotion babe / And they don't know the blues . . ." I thought of how the volcanic steam beneath the city kept everyone alive, but that above ground everyone must sing. Wind pushed a plastic cup along the sidewalk. No one else was walking. The cold and darkness had a purity about them.

We stood outside Laugardalshöllin Stadium, Iceland's largest public indoor arena. The facility held five thousand people—a small number by North American standards. Gary pointed out the enormous banners hanging across the building's glass and steel façade—tropical reds and greens and festive accolades to Cuban culture were everywhere. The building was wrapped tight like a birthday present. I felt odd stirrings of affection—a quiet love for the people of Iceland, who were clearly celebrating the Afro-Cuban soul of a nation. We talked about how Americans would never celebrate the soul of any country by wrapping a public building with praises. The notion was scarcely conceivable. I remembered that when the American musician Ry Cooder produced the first compact disc of the Buena Vista Social Club, the United States government fined him $25,000. Miami's Cuban press had protested the album. It was easy to denigrate the quality of American politics. But still there was something different about the Icelandic joy surrounding this musical visit. We could sense the admiration for the Cuban way of life. It seemed to be a heartfelt thing, unburdened by politics. I wondered if the mood in the concert hall would be different from the concert experiences I'd had before. I thought of having heard Duke Ellington in 1972. The college crowd at the University of New Hampshire was polite but timid, as though the largely white audience felt unworthy to be in Ellington's presence.

Back in the hotel and lying awake for a little while, I heard the harbor wind working at a window frame. The wind and the building made a low moan. I thought about the sense I was having that the people of Iceland were celebrating the Cubans in both personal and collective ways. I couldn't find the words for what I was intuiting, but sinking deeper into my pillow I thought of comic poetry. I felt as though there was something intelligent and playful going on in Reykjavík—the appreciation for the Buena Vista Social Club had something to do with a highly educated public. I recalled George Meredith's essay on comic poetry in which he tries to explain why the art form is so scarce. He said: "There are plain reasons why the Comic poet is not a frequent apparition; and why the great Comic poet remains without a fellow. A society of cultivated men and women is required, wherein ideas are current and the perceptions quick, that he may be supplied with matter and an audience. The semi-barbarism of merely giddy communities, and feverish emotional periods, repel him; and also a state of marked social inequality of the sexes; nor can he whose business is to address the mind be understood where there is not a moderate degree of intellectual activity."

I thought as I drifted off to sleep that I liked this analogy. The Icelandic people were George Meredith's kind of crowd.

The next morning over coffee and rye bread we talked about the compact disc and the documentary film by Wim Wenders that made the Buena Vista Social Club into international stars. I was the only one in our party who hadn't seen Wenders' film. "The film is stunning," Gary said. "The camera moves so slowly over the genteel shabbiness of Havana. You see the chipped paint on the louvered windows. Old cars. Rusted iron balconies. And the sun on everything." Gary poured more coffee into our cups. "And the handsome, dignified face of Ibrahim Ferrer—well he takes the viewer on a tour of the neighborhood in old Havana where all these incredible musicians have been living in silence."

Gary pointed out that Ibrahim Ferrer was the lead male vocalist for the group and said he has the face of a prophet. "As the film unfolds," Gary said, "you meet his musical social club. You see Rubén González, the legendary pianist, and Omara Portuondo, the lead female singer. When she smiles it's like water in sunlight. They will be together tonight at Laugardalshöllin Stadium."

We had some hours to kill before the concert so we piled into our rental car and drove north. We decided to visit Detifoss, Iceland's most famous waterfall. We drove over plains of black volcanic rocks. Occasionally Greg or Gary could see a cottage standing all alone with no sign of its inhabitants. They looked like the upturned and half-buried prows of sailing boats. It was as if they were designed to look like Viking relics. People were still living in half-buried ships under the northern stars.

At Detifoss, the largest waterfall in Europe, Gary and Greg held my arms and guided me down a steep path of worn stones that led to a viewing platform. The roar of the falls echoed off the tall cliffs and the reverberation of falling water created a zone of deep silence. Although we were speaking we couldn't hear each other. Mist fell over our faces and soaked our clothes. I imagined that I'd passed through some portal to the afterlife, what the Tibetans call a *bardo*—I was being led by trustworthy men across a narrow bridge of stones in a roar and mist unlike anything I had ever experienced on earth. I couldn't even hear my own heartbeat, though I could feel the throb of my pulse. My feet slipped on the stones and Greg and Gary held me up. I thought of the first men to visit the falls—the Norse explorers who first found this place. I pictured them standing at the sheer edge of the falls and whipping the air with their bull-roarers made out of bone and sinew. I imagined that when they couldn't hear their own instruments they knew they had found a sacred place. We stood on a broad, flat stone and turned our faces in the drenching mist and felt the power of the falls passing through our bodies as sound waves.

As we drove back to Reykjavík I shivered from the chilling mist and the sense of desolation offered by the falls. I had traveled far north before. I'd been to the top of Lapland where Norway, Sweden, Finland, and Russia all meet above the Arctic Circle. But the barrenness of the Icelandic countryside was more severe than the emptiness of Lapland. I thought of the Agnus Dei: "O Lamb of God, that takest away the sins of the world, have mercy upon us . . ." This was a landscape that called for a kindhearted god. I asked Gary and Greg if they could see any sheep grazing out among the stones. They saw nothing except the hills and the low, gray sky.

The crowd outside Laugardalshöllin Stadium was in good spirits but polite. They reminded me of Finns at the Savonlinna Opera Festival—the assembly was quietly happy and courteous and watching out for everyone's personal space. *If there are pick-pockets in Iceland, they must be very good*, I thought. There was no bumping of strangers. All the talk was soft. The doors would open in half an hour and the throng was around two thousand people. I realized that I was standing in the midst of a very educated assembly. This was in fact George Meredith's kind of crowd. Two men somewhere to my right were talking about the pianist Rubén González. They were comparing him to Oscar Peterson. Behind me a woman was singing gently some lines in Spanish. There was some rhythmic clapping from the back of the crowd. The rhythms were engaging as opposed to being rowdy. The clapping said *Soon we will be inside* rather than *Let us in*. I thought the crowd could be more insistent, it was cold out here. It was the first of May and it might well snow at any time. A woman laughed suddenly with a polished, classy mezzo voice, her good cheer ringing above the people around her. It was a "raggy waltz" we were doing, as Dave Brubeck would say. We were waltzing in place, expectant and ready. Then the doors opened and the crowd surged and I was surprised to see that strangers touched. But they seemed to guide each other rather than push.

We settled into our seats high in the arena. We were in the nosebleed section, though it hardly mattered because the building had an intimate feeling. I told Greg I'd be surprised if it really held five thousand people. But then suddenly the place was full and the volume of the crowd's buzzing increased perceptibly. Someone had thrown a switch. People were bouncing in their seats. They knew what was up. Afro-Cuban proprioception was on the loose. People had been soaking in the volcanic waters and their spleens were wide open for the sexy voice of Omara Portuondo. They were going to get some gold in their veins. Some earthy juice was about to flow. I thought of crowds

I'd been part of. A march in Washington against Nixon and the war in Vietnam; a Frank Zappa concert in Montreal in the dead of winter; my favorite reggae band, Toots and the Maytals, in New York; Carnegie Hall for the tenor José Carreras; Plácido Domingo at the Metropolitan Opera; Bob Dylan on a rainy summer night outdoors; Vladimir Horowitz in Chicago; Jean-Pierre Rampal with the Chicago Symphony; James Galway at Avery Fisher Hall; Stan Kenton and his last big jazz band; Yo-Yo Ma and Itzhak Perlman; the Throat Singers of Tuva . . . Every performance had a characteristic crowd. The people in Montreal who waited for Frank Zappa were viciously drunk. I was only twenty and more than a bit shocked. I'd had this image of Quebec as being something like Switzerland. But the audience waiting on Zappa was a hockey crowd. There were some fistfights. Bottles were thrown among the seats. I tried to think of the smartest crowd I'd ever been in and wondered what I meant by this. I'd never been in an audience where the expectation and discernment and joy of the crowd was as apparent as it was in Reykjavík. A small group of fans sang something from the Social Club's repertoire just a few rows down from us.

Suddenly the assembly leapt to its feet and cheered. The introduction was in Icelandic and I leaned forward hoping that my dictionary knowledge of Swedish would help me figure out what was being said. The president of Iceland was in the house. The Cuban ambassador was being introduced. Everybody was here. I did some quick arithmetic. This crowd of five thousand was to Iceland the equivalent of a crowd of five million in the U.S. In other words, there was no American equivalent for this assembly. They were stomping their feet. The seats were shaking. The man onstage said "Rubén González" and the audience of five thousand erupted like Yankee Stadium during the World Series.

Gary whispered in my ear. "Rubén González is very unsteady on his feet—he has a young woman supporting his arm and they're walking slowly to the piano." The cheering was beyond belief. This was certainly one hell of an admiring nation. It struck me that the Buena Vista Social Club might not have to play a note. They could just stand and wave in the purple stage lighting. And then Rubén González was playing the piano and time stopped. Then he let time back out. He was the sole proprietor of the ticking seconds. One senses this now and then with great jazz piano—Art Tatum could do it. Just stop the clock or let it go like a slingshot, the seconds freed from suspension and flying loose around the hall. And the people hearing this hold their breath or they breathe depending on the actions of a man's hands.

Then a muscular brass section came in. And drums. Bass. The complex cadences of the horns and the staggered tempos of the drums poured out a sound that was intricate and still provided an illusion of simplicity. This was because the horns were more in charge of the melodic line than one supposed at first. I was being happily tricked. Then Rubén González stole the melody back from the trombones. The crowd cheered for the old pianist. The lead trombone player, who Gary tells me looks like a bouncer in a bar, shouted "Ru-bén Gon-zá-lez!" He waved his horn aloft as if some kind of conquest had taken place. But the song wasn't over. Rubén González was playing the piano unlike anyone I'd ever heard. He was Art Tatum but with dark seashells on his fingers.

The audience was roaring once again because Ibrahim Ferrer had appeared. His voice was like smoke pushed through a bamboo flute. He reminded me of the Spanish flamenco singer Camerón. The outer edges of his words revealed an ache that was barely controlled. He was a bird flying in a church. He sang with such heartbreaking simplicity. Like the Fado singers of Lisbon, he was singing of a woman and a city at the same moment. The precariousness of the emotion felt sacred. Just then Ibrahim Ferrer was swaying beneath a stained glass window, pouring out a blues so joyous I had to let go of analogy. Carnegie Hall hadn't prepared me for this man's voice. I took it in with my whole torso. Ry Cooder once said: "In Cuba the music flows like a river. It takes care of you and rebuilds you from the inside out."

Congas were fluttering like leaves before a storm. Then a man's voice shouted: "Omara Portuondo!" The hall was feverish. Maybe it was a dimension of the architecture, but the cheering seemed to be rolling in waves.

Omara Portuondo sang like a woman who had been dancing all night. She sounded like Dinah Washington—sexy and wise. She sang around the melodic lines of Rubén González's piano and a naughty upright bass. I thought of Shirley Horn singing the classic jazz standard "Love for Sale" but this had more shaking going on. Gary leaned in to tell me that Omara Portuondo was wearing an overwhelming sequined gown and showing lots of leg. "She's in her seventies and very sexy," he said. But I didn't need to hear his description. She was bringing the band down behind her. I imagined her pressing downward with her open palms. With absolute possession of time and feeling she shifted the entire hall into a lullaby. She sang an *oggere,* or cradle song, a song steeped in African traditions of the healing arts. She called for a cradle god and her voice was as blue as the Caribbean in winter. The song was part Yoruba mysticism and part Catholic ritual. I remembered that as a teenager whenever I felt especially lonely in my blindness I'd play a 78 record of Xavier Cugat singing one of the best-known Afro-Cuban songs, "Babalu," an invocation to the god of illness. Later Desi Arnaz made the song famous with a highly stylized commercial version.

The songs played by Cuban dance bands often invoke healing. But there are also old blues embedded in their melodies and a complex set of rhythms. In the U.S. the rhythms became more famous than the songs that produced them. Dizzy Gillespie pushed Cuban rhythms into bebop. And suddenly words like "mambo" and "salsa" were everywhere in North America.

Sitting in Iceland, I remembered there were deities behind this music. And there were drums that talk. Bata drums were carried down from the mountains pulsing with shadowy tales of people stolen. The drums talked to any god who could hear. Omara Portuondo sang back and forth with the drummers. There were three discernible pitches from the drums. She worked in and out of the dark trees of these rhythms. She was lost in a forest. Water was falling from a far mountain. *God Almighty*, I thought, *I'm in love. No wonder the Cubans call this woman the fiancée of feelings.*

When the band shifted into a rumba it was because Omara Portuondo had done her work with the gods. We were free to dance now. The rumba took over the hall and the human heat in the auditorium was intense. I smelled perfume all around me. Omara was singing in a low and very seductive register and I realized with boyish wonder that I was becoming aroused. I felt both silly and hot and I sensed that there were thousands around me who were equally feverish. George Meredith was no longer the archetype for this assembly. Walt Whitman was now in the building. An odd, horny hilarity had swept over the crowd.

The audience couldn't let the Buena Vista Social Club leave. The band came out for four encores. The hall thundered with cheering and foot stomping. The judgment of the crowd was only surpassed by spontaneous joy. I realized that I was happier in this crowd than I'd ever been in a public gathering. I hadn't anticipated that this would happen. The rhythms of the percussionist's clave sticks and the vocals and the piano and the spiritual drumming put me in mind of a friend in New York. He once went into a Chinese herb shop in Chinatown and bought dozens of medicinal herbs without fully knowing what he was doing. He brewed these things up and managed to get stoned in a very complicated way. He was wide awake and relaxed. His whole skin felt wildly sensual. Because he didn't know what he'd bought from the herbalist he was never able to duplicate the experience. After the concert, walking outside Laugardalshöllin Stadium, I felt a bit of what my friend must have felt—I had a layered sensation, my brain was unhurried and fast at the same time. I realized while talking with Gary and Greg that I had to lie down. I left them in the lobby of the hotel and headed for bed.

Early the next morning we drove to the Blue Lagoon, a volcanic lake just north of Reykjavík. "It's the world's largest hot springs," Gary said. "It's the crater of a volcano, only now it's a lake filled with hot mineral water." Greg read from a travel brochure. "The mud from the floor of the lake is world famous for restoring youth." "It's mud mask central!" said Gary. "It's Botox crater!" Clearly this was the thing to do before flying home. I could still hear the clave sticks breaking four-four time into rhythm poems behind the voice of Omara Portuondo. I was ready for a mud mask. In fact a mud mask was probably the only thing I was equipped for. How convenient that the Blue Lagoon was on the way to the airport.

We walked from the locker room down to the bubbling shore. Sleet drove in from the north rim of the crater and so we didn't dawdle. At the water's edge we jumped into a lake that resembled an enormous rock-lined bowl of steaming milk. The water along the shore was about a third again hotter than the temperature of the human body. It felt like the first flush of brandy. Gary observed that the water was the color of breast milk. We were floating around the Great Mother's nipple. I drifted away from my friends and felt how the lake grew hotter as I swam away from shore. I dove below the surface and pressed my hands into the volcanic mud. And because I could hold my breath a long time I touched my face to the hot mineral sediment. I heard my heart and knew that I had found a momentary replica of amniotic life. As I swam and pushed my hands into the Delphic sand I heard what I thought at first was a bata drum. I surfaced for air and then dove back down again. I was near the center of the lake. I could hear in the force of the volcanic springs the hollow sound of drums. In Cuba the songs to the gods are played on three different-sized hourglass-shaped batas. One of these drums, called *iyá,* speaks or resonates with the spoken pitches of Yoruba prayers. And there I was, deep in an Icelandic crater, and a wide sound was pushing through my skin.

20. Albatross

———◆———

Old Heiskanen lives in a small place. My friend and teacher the poet Donald Justice would likely have said that Heiskanen comes from a provincial culture. But he's got amazing ears. He has wandered into the city from the Finnish woods. He has immigrated to Sweden and it isn't suiting him well. Poor Heiskanen! He's fled Finland for a Swedish trailer park. If you're not from Finland you might not understand. Nothing is right. The dogs don't bark correctly. No one sings when they're drunk—the Swedes just talk a lot of rot. And the Swedes keep coming up with new slang for things.

Sometimes his Finnish friends cross over on the ferry and tell him he should go home. They fill him with new slang from Helsinki and lots of gossip. And for moments he feels good. He climbs on a rickety chair and sings a folk song about the warming effects of the summer sun. He has a strapping baritone voice.

What's the man's problem? I wondered. *If he's miserable in Sweden, why doesn't he just go home?* Heiskanen was still swaying on his chair and calling to the sun. He had a wide, boozy voice. His friends gathered around and joined in the song.

I was in an outdoor theater in Tampere, Finland, and it was

the week of the summer solstice. I heard Heiskanen climb down off his chair and then I heard his friends clap him on the back and whoop it up. Like all players in burlesque theater, Heiskanen loudly thanked his pals, who were doing the work of the real audience. And the playgoers hastily applauded. There were around five hundred people in the Pyynikki summer theater. The day was suddenly hot and there was a fine breeze off the lake and you could hear the spruce trees and songbirds. And then there was Heiskanen. He had a fine human soul and he was lost in a strange land, though he was lost on purpose or something like that. He knew and didn't know. And the poor man's friends were pure variety-show caricatures. One was a banker. Another was a poet. There was also a sad drunk man from Heiskanen's university days. They were equally full of themselves. And there were several very soulful women Heiskanen was in love with or used to love or would want to love if he could just figure something out.

I wasn't certain about Heiskanen's state of affairs and I was equally confused about my own. I had planned to come to Finland for some summer music. I thought I would practice my listening skills. But instead, sitting there in the open-air Pyynikki theater, I found myself in my own secretive trailer park. I was aware that I'd carved out a provincial place for myself. This wasn't so easy to admit. I was attempting to raise the ante around the art of listening. I wanted to be a listener. And by this I meant I wanted to be a happy man. There. Now I was saying it to myself. What could be more unsophisticated than that? I was an exile from visual culture. I was going to be an advanced ear man in the Scandinavian summer.

Heiskanen's albatross was his own unadorned culture. He was a Finn through and through. This meant that he could sing about being a forlorn island tree and really mean it. His character was modeled loosely on the life of the Finnish popular composer Juha Vainio, who immigrated to Sweden and died there at the age of fifty-two. Vainio has no American counterpart. His songs are standard in Finland in much the way that Woody Guthrie's anthem "This Land Is Your Land" is valued in the U.S. But there's some Noël Coward in Vainio. And some T. S. Eliot. And even a little bit of British music hall vulgarity. And it's entirely a Finnish thing. The irony in Vainio's songs derives from a bipolar split between overromanticizing the world and seeing it for what it is. The contemporary American folk singer Greg Brown sings, "The world ain't what you think it is, it's just what it is." Vainio would add: "The world doesn't need you at all." And this is what Heiskanen must sing about. This is the world of Samuel Beckett, although it's dinner-theater Beckett. Poor Heiskanen in his Swedish trailer park! His assorted friends were waving tropical drinks with little paper umbrellas and laughing way too loudly.

My trouble was that I wanted the world to be something like the Aeolian harp. Or at least I thought I did. I wished for an open door, the wind spilling sound from its treasury. And what the hell did I mean by sound? I meant intelligent sound. What did that entail? I imagined it was sound that carried potential meaning. What did latent meaning mean? Well I guessed it was something you could play with. So I was looking for noises that stirred the imagination. Big deal, I thought. This was what all concertgoers were after. And just then I felt genuinely lonely in that delightful open-air theater. My friend David Weiss was to my immediate right. He spoke no Finnish. I understood just enough to figure out fifty percent of the singing. But things were sung or spoken too quickly for me to translate. Heiskanen and his court were now in the sauna, singing about the ritualized togetherness of women and men in the steam. They laughed like mad because they knew their culture was unrefined. Oh but they were conflicted about it. They were pagans, but then they worried how the world might see them.

I had the feeling that I was both solitary and simple. The sensation had been building for months. I walked around without knowing exactly where I was going and gave myself over to chance soundscapes. Hardly anyone does this, and though you can find writing about soundscapes and the music of what happens, well it's all rather abstract. Sitting in that theater listening to Heiskanen and his friends, I recognized my true situation. I was declaring myself to be a rube. A primeval simpleton. "Now I will do nothing but listen . . ." wrote Walt Whitman. "I hear all sounds running together, combined, fused or following, / Sounds of the city and sounds out of the city, sounds of the day and night . . ."

Thank God for Whitman. What was I so worried about? Heiskanen offered me a reminder. He loves what's primitive about being Finnish. And he hates it at the same time. Suddenly he was singing a song about life and eroticism. Someone shouted "We're in love without a plan!" There was a greasy electric guitar and a heavy-rock drum set. People onstage were staggering around. I thought of Heiskanen's soundscape in all its cheapness and had the sense that the acoustical environment of the popular song was such a frightful prison. Heiskanen wanted the freedom of Nietzsche's Zarathustra, wanted to shape his world and reshape it according to the electricity of inspiration. And now here he was lurching in a circle created by a pop song and bumping into the lawn furniture. Heiskanen was the Finnish version of John Lennon: his ideas were better than his music. Unlike Lennon, the poor guy knew it. Worse still: he had to love the music because it was made from the ambient stuff of his nation, the polka, the nineteenth-century folk songs of liberation, the

lonely hybrid Finnish rock and roll that came of age in the sixties. Poor Heiskanen had been making do with auditory scraps
of popular song. He was a prisoner of sentimental noise pollu-
tion. All he wanted was some poetry. Why couldn't someone just
turn off the radio?

Of course the desire to listen like a romantic is impractical! Who
could live like Rousseau: pretending to be a better man for loving the planet with sharpened ears. Rousseau: who drank Bor-
deaux and nibbled cheese and listened to the insects and
conceived of the mind as a fit tribute to the world.

The Pyynikki summer theater revolved. The audience was
sitting on a motorized set of risers that turned counterclockwise
whenever there was a change of scene. We were sitting inside a
long-playing record, racing from song to song. Heiskanen's story
was mostly a Finnish rock opera. David whispered in my ear
that we were now looking at a crude ballroom. There was polka
music. The Finns love to drink beer and waltz to polka music.
Then the audience was swept by amplified accordion and a four-
four drum. The people onstage danced heavily and stomped
their feet like horses counting numbers in a circus act. And the
audience followed inside the grooves of a 33 1/3 LP that was
spinning backward. Two nights ago in Helsinki I had attended a
Paul McCartney concert under the midnight sun. I remembered
how the Beatles once engineered some of their songs so you
could play the recording backward and hear audible clues about
the rumored death of Paul. This was hot talk in 1968. According
to the gossip industry, McCartney died in May of 1966 while
driving his convertible home after a party. He was most likely
drunk. "He blew his mind out in a car," John Lennon later sang.
"He didn't notice that the lights had changed." On the so-called

"White Album" released in 1968, one could spin "Revolution 9" backward and hear the uncanny voice of a man saying "Turn me on dead man." It was a great publicity stunt, and though the Beatles never acknowledged it, they managed to sell millions of records without going on tour like other rock bands. It was a gold mine. It was a stunt that was tailored for the band's audience. Everyone on both sides of the Atlantic was stoned. Even suburban dentists were taking LSD. And drugs produced provincial culture. Everything was a Masonic sign. McCartney was dead. It was the age of conspiracies and all you had to do was put your record player in neutral and spin the turntable in the wrong direction and you could hear absolute proof that there was some kind of cover-up going on.

Heiskanen was afraid that his nation might be turning into America. And then the theater turned again, and from the adjacent lake came the sound of a motorboat. Friends arrived offshore and told Heiskanen to give up on thinking and have fun. Just change the record. Kick up the mood with a new tune. Don't worry that your local culture has been sold. Don't bother. And you absolutely must give up on this idea that there's a local music. Come on Heiskanen. The man was Hamlet. He was audio Hamlet. He wanted the world to be as it once was. There was something authentic in the past. He can't remember what that was. Oh but rock and roll is here to stay. Come on let's turn Fats Domino over and play the B side. Stop worrying so much. You're only young once.

But there's plenty to worry about, I thought. Cell phones are now so widely used in Finland it's feared that teenagers are losing the ability to speak and write correctly. The kids are addicted to text messaging. They spend hours transmitting shorthand telegrams over the phone and even the government has become concerned that life is being lost from the Finnish language. It is, I suspect, the latest variant of playing the Beatles in reverse. And both of these things are at once harmless and not so harmless. Pop culture and technology drive how people hear, or rather how they don't hear. The audible environment is shrinking.

The ski boat drove off and the theater revolved. Heiskanen sang something about the last day of his life as a metaphor for the next day and the day after that. He really needed to sit down. The theater moved again. We were headed into another song. I thought of the old gramophone I used to play as a boy. I had lots of time to myself as a kid. I spent hours in the attic. The records were all opera arias. In the first two decades of the twentieth century the music industry relied on Verdi and Puccini. Their arias were all about three minutes long and they were perfect for the 78 rpm Victrola. I remembered the machine racing through every disk with spring-loaded vehemence.

Listening to Heiskanen, I remembered the principle of Roman engineering. The three-minute pop song was all that the early Victrola could deliver to living rooms. As any engineer will tell you, the width of a railway axle is the same as a Roman char-ioteer's axle. Later, the European horse-drawn carriages were designed to ride over the rutted roads left behind by the Romans. Finally, railway cars were designed to fit the same specifications. And today Heiskanen and Paul McCartney sing three-and-a-half-minute pop songs. Standard emotion is packaged into syn-copated bursts lasting approximately two hundred seconds. This is Thomas Edison's fault.

The summer theater turned again and we were into a song about traveling north. It was an indisputably Finnish song, but also kind of a Roy Orbison thing. The song was bluesy and made from two hundred seconds of genuine feeling. Heiskanen believed he would find a place to really live. The songs there would be fast because that's how the world was nowadays. He would sing old-time things. He would sing the elevator's music and he would be a careful loser on the pop planet.

21. Letter from Venice

———◆———

I came to Venice precisely because I was blind. The palazzos boasted of sunlight and stood beside the Grand Canal like wedding cakes. Water slapped the boat and somewhere a window opened and I heard a songbird. I guessed it was a Jamaican bluebird. I'd heard him before. A year ago I was standing at the Dunn's River Falls when a Jamaican minister took me by the hand. His palm was rough as a starfish. "Bluebirds sing all around here," he said. "You listen you can hear them above the falls." They were there, talking in the high, sunlit branches.

Now I heard them on the Grand Canal. Then a small girl laughed and a man sang in a baritone voice. I imagined they were on a balcony and waving at the tourists floating beneath them.

Venice has endless distractions for the listener. I'd come here, in part, to prove it. Marsilio Ficino, the Florentine translator of Plato, wrote: *The world is just shapes and sounds.* Ficino said that sound equals form. This poses a challenge—could I, for instance, listen to the accidental music of a place like Venice while my wife explored the architecture? Could I find corresponding pleasure in merely listening?

As luck would have it, my literary agent called while I was pondering this in the New York Public Library. "I have a boondoggle for you," she said. "You can think of it as a romp." What followed was so improbable I could only guess it must be true. A design firm in Milan wanted me to appear in a magazine ad for interior lighting. My memoir *Planet of the Blind* had been translated into Italian under the title *Tutti i colori dei buio* (All the Colors of Darkness). Now the Italians wanted me to pose beneath stylish lights and say: *You can't imagine how I see light.* Of course my wife Connie and I and my guide dog Corky would be flown to Milan. All our expenses would be taken care of. Yes this was a boondoggle . . . Yes they could get us tickets to La Scala . . .

That night sitting in our kitchen Connie and I folded and spindled the journey. I worried about the tactlessness of appearing in an ad for interior lighting. Blindness is not a trifling subject. In my memoir I depict the effects of light and shade as being both shocking and oddly beautiful. My version of blindness still allows me to see colors and shapes, though they are often inexact and more than a little troubling. But forget the aesthetics of the thing: over seventy percent of the blind remain unemployed in the United States. As a blind person I knew it was essential to portray the dignity of physical difference. But I also remembered the American poet Theodore Roethke, who wrote: *The eye, of course, is not enough. But the outer eye serves the inner, that's the point.* I decided that I liked the irony of the advertisement—*You can't imagine how I see light.* This was about the inner eye. Roethke also said: *Literalness is the devil's weapon.* We decided we would go.

My own hearing had become careful and algebraic. If seeing is really an epicurean experience—if a stained glass window can take us higher like the Kama Sutra—then hearing has only its acquired nobility, sequenced and slow. I knew that I needed to go to Venice for "the Ficino Cure." I had to wander in a delirium of sound in a vast city with no cars. I had to get lost there. Connie could go her own way. We'd meet in the evening at Harry's Bar and she could tell me about San Zaccaria and I would tell her about getting lost while following the music of what happens.

First we would go to Milan. The lighting firm had retained the noted photographer Elliott Erwitt to photograph three blind artists. A Russian chess master and a concert pianist from Milan joined me in a villa on the outskirts of the city. Here we were: a crew of blind men who saw light with the inner eye. We were each in his way worried about the dignity of this enterprise. Each wondered if he'd made a mistake. We were upright and quiet. Eventually we were photographed in separate sessions and our paths never crossed again. We were free.

I was surprised by the odor of the stones. The Venetian mortar had a heady scent—the smell of galvanic particles, a chalky smell that was distinct from the ocean.

From the deck of the vaporetto I saw a sack of feathers: tropical feathers, green pastels—then, in the fast-changing light, this became a lemon dessert, a tower of ice—my blindness identified palazzos and clouds through cataracts and damaged retinas and announced that pillows were falling from a great ship. In reality the ship was a church blocking the sun. The pillows were boats piled with produce. "My Venice," it turned out, was a transparency, a slide that had been overexposed, or more properly, two slides that had been fitted neatly across my face. You can't imagine how I see light! Like the poet Wallace Stevens, I was "catching tigers in red weather." Some of the world's most renowned architecture stood before me and I was staring at the protoplasm of microbiology.

I turned to Connie, who is a resolute admirer of sunsets; a café observer—thinking to ask "What's that darkly groomed form over yonder?" but thought better of it for she was in a rapture of the quattrocento. And I, in turn, knew that I must find my own Venice because Marsilio Ficino had challenged me. The light about my head was incandescent, striking. It did not resolve into anything knowable. There was a kind of magnificence about this. I was passing through a prismatic cloud. Venice wore her mask of sea glass and I wore mine. I would dance with her. For music we'd take the ordinary buzz and din of the narrow passageways and canals.

After finding our hotel I made a solo foray into the Venetian alleys. I wasn't exclusively alone since I was accompanied by Corky. Corky was companionable, and unfazed by strange cities. She was also large and handsome with a noble head. Before I'd gone two steps a passing woman remarked: "Cane guida! Bellissima!" I nodded on Corky's behalf and then we sailed up a causeway—man and dog pushed by wind, each of us taking in the aromatic salts and musk of this place we'd never seen before. We turned left and Corky guided me through a medieval warren of slippery paving stones and jutting shops. She hugged the walls, evading a pack of schoolchildren shouting in French. I heard bells from a door, tourists speaking Japanese, and something heavy rolling on casters. The air was wet and cold. I heard caged birds from somewhere above and put out a hand. What was this, a morning glory trellis? I'd backed into a cul-de-sac, a fairy grot, a cave of waterweeds and acacia.

I was in equal parts a figure of struggle and peace; a walking lodestone of sorts. I touched my fingers to a cold window. A fine dust coated the glass. A light rain had begun falling, and since there was no one around I encouraged Corky to relieve herself there in the fairy grot. I stood listening. There were extraordinary songbirds calling from a second-story window. Laughter from above, a woman and a child . . . I couldn't make out the words. Two poets . . . The lyrical push of ordinary Italian . . .

I had to slow down. If I was going to listen to Venice properly I needed to hear the cadences of the place. I needed to stand still. Again I thought of Theodore Roethke: *A poet must be a good reporter; but he must be something a good deal more.* Whitman called this *loafing.* I thought of Whitman observing the parade of humanity with lewd concentration. Walt had a good ear. He loved opera and knew how to sit perfectly still.

At home in New York, Corky and I raced up and down the streets at breakneck speeds. Guide dogs move fast through traffic. We sailed past the expensive couples on their Rollerblades and took the joggers in Central Park by surprise. It was obvious that here in Venice we didn't need to rush anywhere. We could prevail over chaos by means of deliberation.

We trailed the sound of footsteps through a transverse intersection of alleys. Shop bells rang . . . someone opened a door . . . Corky followed a stranger into a shop and we found ourselves in a room full of hand-blown glass. We stood completely still. There was a deep silence. All eyes were watching us. I was certain that the shop's owner was horrified—a blind man with only a dog for company had appeared amid the exquisite glass! We were literally "a bull in a china shop"!

Then there was a noise of little shoes—paper slippers—a tiny person was approaching . . . "Listen," a woman said. I heard the hum of breath moving over glass—she was playing a glass flute! Wind and sunlight pressed through dark leaves. I was sweetly transfixed. This was a shy, unasked-for gift . . . She played the delicate pipe and I imagined leaps of light on water. *A mind of grace is real and it comes by surprise*, I thought. The shopkeeper showed me glass butterflies, a glass cricket, fish, a glass bird with wings outstretched . . .

For the next hour I walked by ear. I broke the rules for the proper use of a dog guide by issuing vague directions, letting Corky wander aimlessly. Together we got good and lost. I tracked the sounds of bells and a scattering of wings and guessed that I'd arrived at St. Mark's Square. It was good not knowing where I was. The sun had come out and a balloon seller walked about in slow circles—maybe he had seeds for the birds instead of balloons. He had a litany of amiable phrases drawn from a dozen languages but none of the words revealed what he was selling. He had a sack of coins that I imagined was hanging from his belt. The coins and the rhythm of his walk were strophe and antistrophe. He sang to the far corners of the square. "Hello! Hello! Beautiful! Beautiful! *Willkommen! Tervetuloa!*" Coins slapped against his belt.

"Are you all right?" The voice was British. Yes, I'd managed to find my way to St. Mark's Square. And Corky was standing stoically amidst thousands of pigeons. The tourists were photographing her.

Apparently a significant number of nuns were snapping our picture. Once the Englishman mentioned it I heard their cameras clicking. I told the Englishman that I was walking and listening with no true destination. He called to his wife. "These two have no idea where they're going," he said. "I mean he's just walking about and listening!" She asked if she could have my photograph. I let them take my picture and then I told them that I must run—it was time to feed the dog.

The sun was setting. I stopped on a bridge and stood for a time. A gondola slipped beneath us, the plash of its rudder sounded like the tail of a pheasant in the grass. I imagined the

gondolier was going home to his wife and children. It was twilight and cold. If he looked back he'd see me leaning on the
bridge and talking to myself. He wouldn't see the dog, just a
man wearing a leather jacket and sunglasses.

Twenty years ago at the Iowa Writers' Workshop I read philosophy like a halfhearted gardener. I sat under willows and
read parts of Kant and Hegel. Now the gondola's hull was
slapping the surface of the canal; the noise echoed under the
bridge. Two women hurried past in the growing darkness; I
could hear them admiring the dog in German. *Guesswork and
understanding create a knowing man*, I thought. *The subjectivity of
Kant . . . Why go anywhere when you can't see? Is it because the
spirit of man and the world of form are identical? Because even with
eyes shut my spirit and the narrow alleys of Venice were one and
the same?*

I listened.

Walked.

Jazz piano drifted from somewhere. There was a nightclub
nearby.

I walked some more.

The Venetians had more caged birds than any other people.

Then I was in a working-class district. The windows of the
apartments were open to spring rain. Radios and televisions
played from building after building. There was a clatter of
dishes . . . I heard a tinny stereo playing the Rolling Stones—
"Jumping Jack Flash" . . . From still another window I heard the
voices of two men arguing. Wild laughter from a woman, a
mezzo-soprano . . . The odd grace of being was in that laugh
because the men stopped—then laughed along with her . . .
They were laughing because twelve moons circled Jupiter . . .
Because one of them had forgotten his left from his right . . .

Hearing poetry starts the psychological mechanism of prayer.
The phrase was Roethke's.
I sat alone in a tiny neighborhood park.
I was amazed at how quiet Venice suddenly was.
It was a city of wind . . .
Someone lowered a flag. There was the unmistakable sound of pulleys. It was time to walk.

Something strange was happening to me. I was surprisingly happy. Why not? I'd been drifting through the unfamiliar atmosphere with only the wind for a map. Was this what happened to sighted people as they wandered in churches and museums?

Corky stopped while I located a flight of steps with my foot. In the distance I heard a crowd. They were still far off. They made a strange buzz. I thought of Samson working his mill.

It appeared that I'd emerged from the vatic silence into a scene of great confusion. I wondered briefly if I'd walked onto a movie set because hundreds of people were shouting in a chorus. I had found my way into the middle of a street protest and I was completely ignorant about what was going on—I was Candide walking among the Bulgarians. Women were shouting. Gunshots rang out. No, they were firecrackers. Corky continued working and guided me through a knot of humanity as if we were in New York at rush hour. She pushed past a group of men who were banging trash can lids. I supposed that the look on my face suggested my incomprehension because someone tapped me on the arm and said: "It's a protest. The hotel workers are going on strike!" There were more firecrackers and then there were police whistles. There was a palpable feeling of anger mixed with hilarity. This was street theater and not a riot. We turned a corner and moved quickly away. I wanted to turn and wave but Corky was going at a good clip.

I wondered if Connie was viewing the paintings of Titian and Tintoretto. Maybe she was drifting in a gondola around Santa Maria della Salute. Me? I was lost. A great baroque weather vane turned before me. Venice—"queen of the seas"—her jewelry and clouds attracting me at random . . .

The next morning I listened on the Bridge of Sighs to the conversations of tourists.

Gondolas floated beneath the bridge.

Leaning at the rail, I overheard a woman talking about her dentist.

"Honest to God!" she said. "You'd think a dentist with his reputation would have noticed by now!"

I wanted to hear the rest, but the Bridge of Sighs swallowed her story.

"It's true!" said a man in another boat. "Just look at the way she dresses!"

"Vitamins," said a different man.

"It's just schoolbook Latin," a woman said.

"The great excitement of Manzoni when Napoleon died," said another woman.

No one noticed the bridge.

"Catherine of Siena," said a man.

"I fully intend to catch up with it!" said a woman.

There were gondolas with nothing but laughing people.

Was it the influence of Disney?

This was the Bridge of Sighs!

The doges of Venice marched their subjects across this span to the waiting prison where they most certainly died from starvation and torture. Later the Austrians marched the Venetians over this same bridge when the Austro-Hungarian Empire owned Venice during the nineteenth century. One can only imagine the Austrians and their efficient cruelties . . .

The gondolas slipped by and the tourists talked in floating zones of contentment.

The gondoliers had completely given up on their traditional role as tour guides. They worked their tillers in silence.

"She was a glowing bridesmaid," said a woman.

There were limits to how much listening I could do without the consoling balance of visual description. Connie took me to the Church of St. Mark's to see the mosaics and I listened as she described the strands of gold finer than hair that were woven through the marble floor.

The tesserae of the mosaic were smaller than chipped diamonds or the microscopic slices of platinum inside Rolex watches.

Connie's voice had a respectful softness. She was a guest. As a result she conveyed her appreciation for the things she saw.

We stood in the great church amidst a billion inlaid fragments of glass, marble, and tile.

Later we drifted through the city. Connie described the Rialto Bridge. With its baroque foppishness it looked temporary—as if it was erected for a wedding.

We saw Mozart's louvered window. The building was in the dark even at midday.

We saw a canal that had been dammed at both ends and then drained. Men were working at the foundations of a sinking palazzo with what appeared to be rubber mallets.

We noticed a horse on a thin bridge, improbable as an onion atop the queen's crown.

Three men wearing black tuxedos waved from a motorboat.

We drifted around the Church of Santa Maria della Salute. Gulls rose and fell against a backdrop of dark Adriatic clouds.

Lights appeared at the tall windows of the monastery.

We sat above the Grand Canal and sipped wine. The Venetian dusk called the bleached whiteness out of the stones. I talked about listening as a variation of sight-seeing. Connie was a professional trainer of guide dogs. Accordingly she knew a good deal about the art of hearing. More than once while training her dogs she assumed the role of a blind person by walking blindfolded through the streets of New York. As Huck Finn would say, "she has sand."

My Olympiad was to find aesthetic pleasure among the riches of the baroque with little or no visual help. The trouble with this plan was glaringly obvious—the sounds of a place were products of random nature—they were happenings of luck and factors of wind. Boats turned at their moorings. There was music from their chains. A window slid open because a little boy saw a calico cat on a ledge—the cat who got away last night—and now the boy was calling softly. This was the mysterious aleatoric work of the hourglass. But no listener could ever hear in the wind the exquisite formal arrangements of architecture. For this I would always require help. And something more—a nobility of descriptive engagement from my wife and from my friends . . .

The next morning Connie spotted a motor launch piled high with boxes of Jaffa oranges. The boat was in the hands of a single man who believed that with mind over matter he could squeeze his cargo beneath a miniature bridge. Connie described him as he drove his tower of crates into a mousehole. There was a groan, then a splintering of wood. The people atop the bridge broke into rowdy laughter. Salty, colorful words boomed back and forth. One man shouted: "The bridge is too slight for such a thing. Back up!" All the while the reckless captain worked feverishly to break the logjam. He kicked at crates of oranges and three of them tumbled into the canal where they bobbed like deck chairs thrown from a stricken ship. Now the crowd on the bridge shouted more instructions. "You need additional weight! We'll come down!" Four stout men climbed over the railing of the bridge and dropped into the flimsy motor launch. They lay down on top of the crates. They were willing the boat to sink lower. The captain prodded the ceiling of the bridge with his skinny arms. "If the canal rises they'll be stuck in there," said Connie. "I wonder if the Venetian water patrol carries the Jaws of Life?"

We watched as five men laughed their way under a bridge. Heft and hilarity were their only tools of navigation.

Had I been walking alone I would have missed this splendid moment. The predominance of the eye—that old magician! How he snaps us to attention whenever he discovers chaos. A friend calls on the phone and says: "I just saw the damnedest thing! A white cloth seemed to be dancing by itself under the trees. For a minute I thought it was a ghost. When I looked again I saw it was a squirrel with a man's handkerchief in its mouth."

The "willing suspension of disbelief" is the very faith of poetry, as Coleridge said. But it's also a prime ingredient in the gleam of the eye. I don't think it really matters whose eyes are gleaming. As long as my companion is a talkative enthusiast of the odd apparition, everything will be okay. I can know the world by proxy.

Walking in Venice in long, slow circles, I realized that sound is to shape as thirst is to hunger. Ficino understood the nature of the meal.

Dear Marsilio Ficino,

I travel with my wife. And yes, she sees better than 20/20. Ted Williams, the baseball player, also had 20/10 sight. In his heyday with the Boston Red Sox he saw the stitches on a fastball. Connie sees blackbirds flick their wings in the corn of southern Ohio. She drives at seventy miles per hour and notices red squirrels, pheasants, bob-headed quail, Arabian horses . . . Handmade signs for Ohio Swiss cheese, sausage, fresh dill pickles . . . In Venice she spots the unhistorical shops selling faux zebra hides—"in case you need to cover your piano," she says . . . And the shop displaying handmade women's shoes, but only for the left foot, a specialty trade . . .

And yes, dear Ficino, Connie reads me the menus in comic Italian, and the waiters look on with contempt—but their scorn turns to dismay when I tell them we're only ordering for the dog. And in turn we walk the palazzos with Corky heeling beside us and I see the interiors that Connie sees, hear her voice among the dazzling arches and feel that I have stepped through a thin wall of sleep into someone else's dream. And this is all right. Why not? We train all our days in the geometry of self so as not to get lost. Why not get lost in someone else's wonder?

On our last morning in Venice I went out alone. The air was bluish in my retinas . . . Trees clicked in a small park. A frenzied Pekinese followed me. He barked like a motorized winch in need of oil. He was a stray. There were strays all over Venice. *Once*, I thought, *they lived in the palaces.*

I walked. It was early and shopkeepers swept and launches delivered goods. Once more I was in no remarkable spot, I was merely standing beside a weathered door. I pressed my palms against the wood. It was rough as pumice, or the barnacled hull of a New England dory. Sometimes I believe that beneath the rutted surfaces of wood I can feel the grain, the pith of the tree. This was a black oak from Macedonia. In my mind's eye I could see where it stood on a great estate— saw the picnickers beneath it, some five hundred years ago.

22. A Day of Fast Talk in Columbus, Ohio

"I'm so angry!"

The voice was a man's: middle-aged with gravel in his windpipe.

"I'm so angry!"

He swayed in the aisle of the bus, hands free, heavy feet dancing.

I nodded and put my arms around my dog guide, who was resting his head on my knee.

Before the angry man had a chance to say anything else, a woman to my left who was holding a mildly fussy baby said: "My boyfriend's in prison but when he gets out tomorrow we're getting married." I didn't know who she was addressing. But the angry man knew. He swayed on those enormous feet and I knew he was looking her up and down. Suddenly he said: "I could cook you something!" He said it as though these were his first words to a woman after a long sea voyage among men. There was something horrifically cheerful in his tone. "You could come over to my house and I'd cook you something you've never had before! Have you ever had fried pancreas?" he asked. "I do a mean pancreas." The baby fussed. I thought it had a pacifier in its mouth.

The woman, a girl really, she sounded like she was about sixteen, said: "My boyfriend's getting out of jail tomorrow and we're getting married."

"That don't mean you couldn't come over to my house for some pancreas," said Angry Man.

I was thinking there was booze involved in this but I didn't smell liquor.

"I gotta buy a wedding dress tonight," said the girl. And Angry Man said: "Well if you change your mind here's my address." He handed her a piece of paper.

And then he was gone.

He bolted off the bus at a stop called "Park of Roses" and I pictured him hunting for rose hips under a shaggy trellis— something sweet to add to his pancreas should the girl change her mind.

Then she turned my way, shouldered the infant, and said: "My fiancé is getting out of prison tomorrow and we're getting married right away."

I was thinking that anger and hunger are probably the same word and then I realized I had to say something so I said: "Can you imagine eating pancreas without mint jelly? I mean, he didn't mention the condiments!" And lucky for me we were at my bus stop and I said goodbye and my dog and I lumbered for the door.

Walking the sidewalk, I thought: *hunger, anger, wedding dress, prison, fried pancreas, mint jelly, prison, hunger, anger, dress, pancreas* . . .

I was moving south on High Street, directly opposite the campus of the Ohio State University. The neighborhood was a warren of beer joints and tattoo parlors and burrito shops. I heard coins in a cup. A woman blocked my way. My dog had stopped in his tracks. He couldn't see a way to get around her. The coins rattled like BBs in a can.

"Can you help me out?" she said. "I haven't eaten in days and I'm not from around here."

Her voice was like darkened sand.

Before I had a chance to answer, a man's voice said, "Keep moving, lady," and I heard the squawk of a radio and guessed that he was a cop. And then wind blew as if it had been released from the opened bag of the wind god and leaves whirled about us in a macabre dance and newspapers sailed along the sidewalk, and behind these not-so-innocent sounds I heard the woman's voice persisting, "I'm hungry and I'm from out of town . . ."

Again the cop told her to keep moving. She said, "I'm from out of town," as if he hadn't heard. A college kid rumbled past on a skateboard. The woman and the cop and my dog and I were all in the white desert of rhetorical hunger in Columbus, Ohio. We were dark humanoid figures in a frameless window.

The cop believed that the woman was harassing a blind guy. This is what I imagined anyway. He thought that because I was blind I was an easy mark. His voice was more impatient than it should have been.

"C'mon," he said with a frayed insistence. "Get moving right out of here!"

I wanted to say that she was okay. She was okay with me. I wanted to tell the cop that an elemental and fast-burning thread runs through every human life—that the cop's life will be changing before he knows it, that nothing can alter this.

Instead I said that I had some money for this woman. I said that I'd been hungry before. I said that asking strangers for money is what churches do. I talked fast and thrust a ten-dollar bill into the woman's cup and said to the cop that he needed to help me find the crosswalk and then he found himself escorting me because he was facing a crowd of passersby and what else was he going to do?

As we walked together I told the cop that no one knows who is really hungry and who is merely saying it. I told him that's why Jesus fed everybody. He must have thought I was a holy roller. In fact I was just trying to distract him from hassling a woman begging change on a day of unpredictable wind. We got to the crosswalk. I said to the cop some lines from the Peruvian poet César Vallejo: "Spring will come. You'll sing 'Eve' / from a horizontal minute, from a / furnace where the spikenards of Eros burn."

I was guessing the woman with her cup of coins was out of view. I was talking without pausing like everyone else I'd heard that morning.

23. The Twa Corbies

———◆———

As I was walkin' all alane
I heard twa corbies makkin a mane
Tha tain unto the other ane say-o
"Where sall we gang and dine the day-o
"Where sall we gang and dine the day?"

The boy next door has learned how to create piercing whistles
with a blade of grass and tells me he can get the attention of
crows and blue jays. He's just a kid in suburban Columbus,
Ohio, a ten-year-old who plays too much Nintendo, but now he's
delirious because he's got the birds talking. He stands under a
locust tree and blows. A loud crow struts a telephone wire and
calls back.

I picture Yamaguchi Goro playing the shakuhachi flute in the
woods of Nara. Music, even a child's primal music, pays homage
to the soundscape. When I was a kid we lived on a dirt road in
New Hampshire. The crows and blue jays walked across our roof
and fought like mad. We were an anomalous family out there in
the woods. We practiced a kind of ersatz Zen—risking silliness
with the crows and talking back to everything that called.

When I was a kid and living in those woods I was in love with Bessie Smith's voice. It sprang from the record player—a voice that could pound nails. God how I loved her! I loved when the song came to an end and the needle drunkenly bobbed against the label. And the ghost of Bessie's voice still circled around me.

I fished through stacks of acetate records. What an odd assortment! Dinah Shore's "Mother May I" and Amelita Galli-Curci singing in *Carmen;* Furtwängler conducting the Berlin Philharmonic; Bix Beiderbeck and Tommy Dorsey. Strangest of all was a group of records from the Soviet Union—martial music performed by the Red Army. The labels in Russian revealed nothing about their mysteries. One could hear the Stalinist fervor of a thousand men with arms linked, men marching across Kazakhstan.

I spent the better part of the summer of 1959 listening to records or walking the woods, where I thought I might find the singing soldiers of the Red Army. Instead I found the crows.

Every summer I return to New Hampshire. I climb a steep hill on the north side of Rattlesnake Island. I'm lucky to own a cabin "out" on the lake. Lake Winnipesaukee is the largest lake in New England and from its shores you can see the White Mountains and the Ossipee Range. Even though I'm blind I often come alone to the island with only my dog for company. I listen to lightning storms and fierce waves. Sometimes I wake before sunrise and the lake is still. This morning two crows are talking. Where have I heard them before? Mozart's *Die Entführung aus dem Serail*—Konstanze and Blonde—Edita Gruberova, and Gösta Winbergh laughing, contralto, atrocious and beautiful. I realize that my first job of the new summer is to listen to the crows all day.

There's a Korean saying that the crow has twelve notes, none of them music. Not so! These crows down by the lakeshore

are D-flat and F. I take a tuning fork and place it against a dou-
ble-pane glass window. These operatic crows are making notes.
They are each performing a recitative, gloating over the entrails
of a gull . . . talking about the hint of rain in their respective trees
. . . Or maybe like Walt Whitman they are singing of

> *My respiration and inspiration, the beating of my heart, the*
> *passing of blood and air through my lungs,*
> *The sniff of green leaves and dry leaves, and of the shore and*
> *dark-color'd sea-rocks, and of hay in the barn . . .*

At sunrise when the lake is still the crows are pulsing with songs.
I won't say they are making harmony. To the human ear the notes
of the crows are dissonant. The cochlea in the human head is
stretched too tight to hear anything like consonance from the birds.

I taught at a small college for nearly a decade. One semester I was
assigned a classroom next to the resident neuropsychologist's lab-
oratory—a room that was originally a corner of an attic. While
my students talked about the work of poets like Mary Oliver and
Kenneth Rexroth, men in the adjacent lab were busily removing
small sections from the brains of parakeets. It turned out that these
researchers could stop the birds from singing. This was a small
college mind you. I suspect they were trying to look lively, men
and boys in lab coats and clutching forceps.

Birds without song are no longer capable of "birdness."
They simply sit in their cages like ripening figs. Open the doors.
They still sit and ripen. "Hell," I said, "you might at the very
least have made them tone-deaf." Even singing badly has its
pleasures . . .

———

Of course this is ridiculous! A blind man stomping off to the forest to listen to the unmusical corvidae—the ugly crows . . .

A blind guy with a tuning fork under the birch trees and pines of New Hampshire . . .

Like Chuang Tzu, he'll recognize that "heaven and earth possess great beauty and use no words . . ."

I find a grove of spruce trees. My name in Finnish means "grove of spruce"—I'm sitting in my own totem. I've crawled through a spider's web. My hair crisscrossed with spider silk and dead bugs. I've wriggled into a nest of childhood.

As a visually impaired kid who played no baseball, I spent a thousand hours in places like this. I learned how to spin a story in a sheltered place. Writers are all orphans of a kind. Of course. But I learned my listening early. Knew the cicadas from the katydids. Knew starlings from grackles. And so here I am, covered with mosquito repellent, my head resting against the hairy trunk of a spruce.

I hear a branch squeaking. Dry old wood in a dry climate. Sound of an old man's knees . . . The sound of oars along the Nile . . . First sound of ancestor worship . . . One night while housesitting the farm for a writer in Iowa I put a log on the hearth and heard an unearthly crying from the old wood. It lasted a good ten minutes. I was alone in a strange farmhouse, twenty miles from the nearest town. I shivered. Understood Shamanism . . . the belief in metempsychosis starts with fire . . . It's later refined by the German mystics—Jacob Boehme, avatar or conductor of the Lord's electrolysis, the spirit of God flowing invisibly through everything . . . And so onward to Carl Jung and Shirley MacLaine . . .

Under the spruce I hear a clicking . . . a sound of knitting needles . . . old crone with her skein of yarn . . . what is that?

It dawns on me that I'm listening to the crows' beaks!

Forget Ted Hughes with his Miltonic crows shouting about the darkness between stars—the crows are watching me and working their beaks in code—a sound like buttons thrown against glass . . .

How do I know the clicks are from the crows? Rhythm and pitch. Crows talk sotto voce and the sounds they emit occur at a leisurely frequency—sound of a child with two small sticks, a child with something else to think about, a child who forgets percussion and then returns to it . . . Crows at the summer solstice preening among dark branches . . . I hear a woodpecker just north of our position—our position—me and the crows . . .

The woodpecker, voracious, works at a dead maple tree— the woodpecker makes a sound like popping corn. Hell, he wants to burn down the house, throw the baby out with the bathwater . . . he lacks all dignity . . .

Wind pushes through the pines.

It's a mariner's sound.

And now events in the woods start to happen quickly.

As near as I can tell there are two crows above me. Now a third arrives emitting shrill cries—a scree of crow aggression . . . It's as if he was driven here by the wind. For analogy the movement is from allegro to vivace . . . fast, dark, and violent chords from a piano . . . I'm sitting under a crow fight!

How did I find these crows in the first place?

What brought me to just this spruce?

Humility I think.

A. Walk blindly into the woods.

B. Concentrate on the ground.

C. Give attention to the branches swaying at eye level.

D. Crawl on your belly through the needles and dry leaves.

E. Locate a trunk where you can rest your back.

F. Be mindful that the crows have a place in this sector. I mean listen before you crawl.

G. Keep your mouth shut.

H. Stay in the same place for five hours.

How engrossing! The crows fighting . . . The crows in the spruce are householders. Crow interloper assails and the homesteaders respond noisily. They sound like diamond cutter's drills—forget "cawing," this is amplified needle-nosed precision, hard forces pitched against an equally hard strength. And there's plenty of bluster. Crow interloper wants to devour the householder's eggs. Crow interloper will eat anything in the world, living or dead. Crow interloper was last seen flying along the lakeshore with a dead snake in his beak. For dessert he picked the eyes out of a dead perch. He'll eat guano and grasshoppers. Spiders. Fireflies. He'll eat the twine off a farmer's scarecrow and the electrical wiring strung outside the barn. He eats dropped pennies. Now he plans to eat the eggs of his kin.

Wind and the battle cries of three crows . . .

And now the woods are filling with the cries of their neighbors!

What wonderful dark screams!

From my recess under the spruce I try to estimate how many are calling. I have to listen for duration in their calls. They talk over each other. Start over again. Change direction. Pitch alters. New ones join the group. It isn't a chorus. Don't call it that. In popular parlance this is called a "murder" of crows—a gathering when dozens of crows will speak. No wonder the farmers of old Scotland thought of witchcraft when they heard this dark mother-scream from the woods! How many are here? Approximately twenty crows surround me.

Did Pythagoras derive his scales from the cries of birds?

Probably not . . . But I hear consonance in the riot. It just so happens that they are making notes. Just as heavy machinery or rainwater in a tin dish will make notes. But it's the one-upmanship of the crows that suggests a primitive musical scale. Ah the crows and mathematics! The crows savoring something dead and bragging about it . . . And the crows defending their nests . . . And the bullyboy crows . . . The hieratic calls from across a ridge of trees . . .

Appetites and a spirit of defense determine the music that comes about . . .

According to Aaron Copeland, informed music listeners listen on three planes. The first hearing is "sensual"—we're made aware of a note—the wind chime of the sailboat's rigging—clatter of tackle in A minor . . . The "expressive" plane comes next—the result of composition—there's some kind of meaning behind the composer's score. Many a listener has foundered on this coastline! Finally there is the "musical" plane—the specialty of trained musicians whose concentration rests on the intricacy of an arpeggio or the parallel structure of melodic lines written for instruments in conversation.

I'm listening to a crow fight. There are notes. And circles of expression grow outward like rings in the water. And circles collide—urgencies of crow make a wider dissonance . . . The noise of a bird fight begins on the sensual plane but it cannot be heard on a "musical" plane—this is the liberation of the thing—the crows are fighting but they're not composing anything; their outbursts are musical at the level of sensuality. Dumb notes. Rocks dropped in a well . . .

Crow interloper has been driven off. The "murder" chorus

and the defensive position of the householders did the job. Crow interloper sails now above the deciduous trees that grow along the shore. He will steal a red ribbon from a straw hat. I'm still motionless under the spruce. The crow fight can be understood on the expressive plane—even though the score was unwritten. Even though the crow fight chorus is aleatoric, a thing of chance created by wind and sudden appetites . . . even so it's the music of "intentionality." Even the lab boys with their scalpels would agree. Call it instinct. Call it avian pique. Notes occur. They stand for real business.

A daddy longlegs scuttles through my hair.

A small something moves through the leaves to my right.

I think how the genome composes the crow's chorus. The elder-hand moves in the buzz and spark of molecular spin.

The music of multiplication is squeezed from the crows. And chaos theory tells us exactly when the crows will sing. But it can't predict the notes. There is nothing like harmony from the spruce grove. And without harmony I hear the soundscape of warring birds—the notes pushed like steel shavings in the magnetic darkness.

My friend Dave, a writer with a good ear, calls in the evening looking for reassurance that I haven't broken my neck. I tell him about my early days when I listened to the Red Army on the Victrola. How I'd put my head in the iron stove to hear a chorus of crickets. I tell him that sitting for the songs of the crows is the most natural thing in the world. "It's not so bad to be blind and alone in the woods," I say. "The only tricky part is finding my way home without the dog. I leave him behind because he scares the birds."

Without the dog it takes me an hour to cover a hundred yards of forest. I keep my hands out and wear lab goggles. I wear thick boots. I call back to the magpies and a catbird. I talk back to a tree frog. And far off I hear the roar of water.

24. *Skull Flowers*

———◆———

— FOR BRENDA BRUEGGEMANN

I sit all afternoon in a low-slung canvas chair and keep still because I can hear the blue heron tracking mice through pond grass. It is good just sitting here. My ears know the sky, the opaque and impossible air is filled with purple feathers— martins catch mosquitoes even in a light rain. Twilight brings them. I listen to the hum of gnats. I hear the crickets and the thin call of a whip-poorwill.

Human ears stand like dried flowers. The pinna, the twin flowers of cartilage, dry, without much blood, they hang out there, transparent crescent moons. The purple martin drops from the barn's roof quick as a flying mongoose, dropping fast as gravel in a well. And air, obedient, moves with him, and molecules are pressured, and the vibrations rush into my dried flowers. The cartilage shakes, hot sounds reach the brainstem faster than the purple martin can swallow the errant hornet. The pars tensa, the ear's receiving membrane, is quicker than all the wrapped tissues of the brain. And now I am leaning far to the left in my chair, pushing these skull flowers into the fast air. And my ears leverage the molecules, ratchet the force upward through the long mystery of bones and canals, in effect slingshoting the molecular vibrations deep in the brain. Fast as the martin devours his insect, the sound is faster still as it passes through the chambers of the ears, those little Franciscan rooms . . . and finally the racing molecules of pushed air—all generated by the martin's evanescent wings, reach the cochlea, that snail where microscopic hairs lift and fall in a fabulous dance . . . Imagine a writhing hairy blanket, a blanket on the back of a shivering horse . . . and the hairs send a sound like crystals falling together, or tuning forks dropped in mathematical precision . . . This is the wild, auditory language of the brain itself . . . I sway in my camp chair . . . now it's getting dark and a thunderstorm is coming . . . The storm is far off, booming with a call to the obdurate flesh. The storm enters my ears. The root hairs of the cochlea sway and spark.

25. Subway

—————◆—————

—FOR JOHN D'AGATA

New York: Number 4 train to Brooklyn.

Woman with knitting needles.
"Nice dog," she said.
"Thanks," I said.
"I had a dog like that once, but someone poisoned it."
The train shuddered at a turn in the tracks. For a moment all one heard was protesting metal under the floor.
Then, again, the tick of her needles . . .

26. *A Lakeside Meditation*

———◆———

All morning it rained and the lake was dark and I don't know why, but I thought of the minute or so in *Hamlet* when the gravedigger gets to be the poet. No one else in the play gets to be the poet: forget Rosencrantz or Horatio or Ophelia. Poets believe in irrational grace. Outside birds called over the water. I thought that if the rain stopped I'd go to the shore and pick berries or stand in the wind for just a little while.

The gravedigger in *Hamlet* digs a grave and holds up a skull and manipulates the jaw. Last spring when my father died we forgot somehow to hire a minister for the interment of his ashes and I was asked to speak. My mother was there and my sister and my father's oldest friends. Standing in the April snow of New Hampshire, I wanted to reassure them, wanted some words of consolation. I stood in the frozen cemetery and recited lines from Whitman:

> *What do you think has become of the young and old men?*
> *And what do you think has become of the women and children?*

They are alive and well somewhere,
The smallest sprout shows there is really no death,
And if ever there was it led forward life, and does not wait at
the end to arrest it,
And ceas'd the moment life appear'd.

All goes onward and outward, nothing collapses,
And to die is different from what any one supposed, and luckier.

When I stopped reciting, the word "luckier" tipped in the
wind and flew unsteadily, as young birds often will. I stood in
the living self and heard the dry winter leaves in the oaks and
birches. I heard the blue jays and crows calling. I felt the terrible
simplicity of listening and that word "luckier" still flying.

It was very quiet.

I remembered that my father was both hardworking and
funny.

It was luckier then. Three blue jays began to fight high in
the birches.

Blue jays were fighting and drill-dancing in the trees.

They are perfect talkers, blue jays. Each gets his turn to
exult or protest, which is to say their cries accomplish both. And
each waits for the other to finish his call before starting his own.
All goes onward and outward in perfect time.

So it went that afternoon. Luckier. Blue jays. Disordered.
Measured.

27. *Inside the Fence: Baseball and Blindness*

— in memory of David Citino

"It's Ozzie's legs," says the beer man. "I swear the guy's got legs like Slinkys! He dances off first on these goddamned bouncing legs and it drives Carlton totally nuts!"

The beer man smells like mentholated shaving cream and he chews Juicy Fruit and his false teeth click and he's breathing heavy. I reach out and touch one of his forearms. He's holding the aluminum tray of beer cups and ignoring the cries of the beer drinkers. He has seen my white cane, this beer man. He ignores his customers. Somewhere behind us a man cries out, "Beer for chrissakes! Whaddya blind?"

"Pardon me," says the beer man—MY beer man—"but can I borrow your cane?" He waves the cane in the direction of his tormentor. "Yeah I'm blind, you two-bit piker!"

"Carlton isn't going to last the inning. Ozzie's ruined his concentration."

The beer man shuffles away.

I've always thought of baseball as being essentially a farmer's invention: the field laid out in such a way that both the players and spectators must scan the horizon. We look up from our plowing; see the mackerel skies sweeping in from the prairies.

It's a game of close work, then a game of visionary staring.

Between extremes of the eye, however, baseball is a game of talk. It owes its lineage to village gossip. Somewhere between the nearly invisible shift of clouds above the infield and the subtle shift of outfielders before the next pitch, somewhere a fan, man or woman, turns to another man or woman and says, "The McGrath house burned last night."

And the impossibly slow pitcher leans forward on the mound like an old farmhand inspecting the cow's udders. The pitcher's ass is thrust backward, his center of gravity counterbalanced against the forward thrust of his hips. He's leaning strategically, poised to leap backward should the great, imaginary animal choose to kick.

The pitcher stays in this position far longer than our hip flexors will usually tolerate. There's plenty of time for gossip.

Blind and always eavesdropping, I've actually heard the following things at ballparks:

"You should have seen how those people lived! I mean it was a carnival out there. The house full of tropical birds. Egrets. Peafowl. And the birds walked all over the furniture." *(This was a male voice, polite. Olympic Stadium, Montreal, Canada.)*

"Let's jump in the car, honey, and drive all night. Headaches don't last so long west of the Rockies." *(Male voice, all buttermilk. Comiskey Park, the old Comiskey, Chicago, Illinios.)*

"Jesus! The ball handcuffs him, bounces off his chest—and the runner runs into it! Shit, I could do that!" *(Man, baritone. Fenway Park, Boston, Massachusetts.)*

"My uncle, the one from Germany, owned a Buick Riviera

and he used to wash it with Rheingold beer." *(Woman, high and impulsive. Shea Stadium, Flushing, New York.)*

"Venner calls the electrician, who rips out all the wiring. I mean they're trying to find the hum, right? But Venner's got ten thousand bees in the attic! The electrician never goes up there because Venner says the attic's not electrified. Shit! You should've heard that electrician when he finally went up there! They heard him all over Ocean City!" *(Man, Brooklyn accent. Shea Stadium, Flushing, New York.)*

"If you don't mind . . ." (She's in her twenties—drunk, swaying, I can hear her swaying . . .) "If you don't mind, I mean it's kinda personal, but why do you go to a baseball game if you can't see?"

"Oh, it's easy," I say. "The dog watches the game."

"C'mon!" says her boyfriend. He pulls her toward the escalator. Her voice rises with the automatic stairs. "Can you believe it? The dog watches the game!" *(Safeco Field, Seattle, Washington.)*

The radarman at Shea Stadium tells me that the hundred-mile-per-hour fastball is a fiction. "No human being can really throw a baseball that fast," he says. "The radar is clocking the last second when the ball swerves. If a man could throw a ball a hundred miles per hour, he could also lift a Chevrolet off the ground with one hand."

I don't like hearing this. I want baseball players to be godlike. There's something in this guy's voice, a nasal and supercilious resolve that reminds me of those guys in high school who bragged about their stereo equipment and used words like "impedance" and "amperes." Guys who never got laid.

He's perfect. A conspiracy theorist. Can't talk during the

game. Hunches over the radar gun. Clocks Randy Johnson's fastball. Plays guardian of the secret.

I don't have the heart to tell him that when a baseball dips or swerves it's actually losing velocity. He's happy in his nominal world.

"Hey, Popeye! Don't ever come back to Boston! We'll kill you slow!" *(Yankee Stadium, Bronx, New York. Fan, belligerent, possibly drunk. Shouting at Don Zimmer, Yankees third-base coach. Former manager, Boston Red Sox. Believed responsible for Boston's loss in 1986 World Series.)*

My father was a dyed-in-the-wool, deeply masochistic Boston baseball fan. Once when we were leaving Fenway Park together after a particularly unbearable loss to the Yankees, he quoted W. H. Auden's poem "Musée des Beaux Arts," in which "someone else is eating" while calamity befalls poor Icarus.

He turned to me as we pushed our way through the departing crowd in Kenmore Square. "You know who the 'someone else' is in that poem?" he asked. "Those are the Yankee fans."

Two women at Yankee Stadium talk during the mid-game lull. There's a moment in every baseball game, no matter how large the crowd, when the entire stadium seems asleep. The people fold into themselves in the great cone of light that is the park. The crowd murmurs in sleep.

"I told him he's losing the kind of woman who can save the world—that is, if anyone can save it."

"Does that mean you?" says woman two.

"Well, it's not the bimbo!"

The game goes on in a separate universe.

I like getting to the stadium early while batting practice is taking place. I love the fat sounds of baseballs thrown and caught and baseballs smacked and the loose banter of ballplayers dipping and turning amid lazy or berserk baseballs and the sun beating down a little too brightly. Kids lean out waving balls and programs for the players to sign. "Come on Mike, have a heart! Have a heart!" cries a kid, a boy, probably around twelve years old. He's almost a big kid. He shouts: "Hey Mike, c'mon Piazza, I only got one day this season!"

The security guard tells me about the weird stuff they find in the men's room.

"Found a German Lugar in a toilet."

"Found brassieres, more than once."

"Found a Chihuahua."

(Old Municipal Stadium, Baltimore, Maryland.)

Now and then I interrupt my eavesdropping and listen with earphones to the sportscasters. The smoky assurance of their voices makes the crowd disappear. Or to put it another way, the crowd goes on with its ignoble chatter while the radiomen turn the game into a thing that has nobility—maybe the word is "credence." Suddenly the game has the elements of tragedy: it has complete action and the proper magnitude. And the announcers use also Aristotle's favorite weapon: the adornments of language. They present the game in a dramatic form rather than a narrative one. The pitcher "deals"—the game is now poker. As the ball leaves the pitcher's hand the card falls on the table, facedown. Everything rides on this. The batter has wagered his house. Still, I think it's safe to say that only a quarter of the crowd is paying attention. A guy behind me is talking about the mayor of New York, whom he clearly doesn't like. This man is not thinking about the six elements of tragedy. He is not looking at the field. He doesn't hear the radioman say that "the outfield is straightaway and the runners will be going on the next pitch. Every base is full and the count is 3 and 2." So there are two games taking place this afternoon at Shea Stadium. For the man who hates the mayor the game is merely a slow narrative like a fishing trip. But there is also Aristotle's game taking place inside the radio.

Plot. Character. Diction. Thought. Spectacle. Melody.

Plot: Aging pitcher returns from Tommy John surgery.

Character: Warrior.

Diction: Can't overpower with the heater; has to throw junk.

Thought: He has studied with the great Calydon of Pelops, wiliest of pitching coaches . . .

Spectacle: Walks around the mound between pitches; takes off his hat; digs a trench around the pitching rubber with his foot . . .

Melody: "He delivers and there's a high fly ball, deep to center, way back—and you can raise the window, Aunt Minnie, here she comes!"

(Fenway Park, Boston.)

Two students from MIT watch the game on acid . . .

They assure me the Boston pitcher, Pedro Martínez, sheds strands of iridescence: long moonglow strings of light as he throws . . .

At Safeco Field in Seattle two men argue about rock and roll:

"Shit, if Bo Diddly's not in the Rock and Roll Hall of Fame, what makes you think P. Diddy is going to get in?"

I can't hear the other guy, there's a roar from the crowd.

My friend Michael has gone to get garlic French fries.

Now the opening riff of Jimi Hendrix's "All Along the Watchtower" rockets through the ballpark. This is Hendrix's hometown.

Baseball is now fully merged with rock and roll. The organ that once played with such proper and solemn patience is gone. Each batter has his favorite song cued up on the vast sound system. The ballpark has become a kind of amplified pinball machine.

This wouldn't matter except that baseball is really a funereal game. It's a kind of Roman funeral: the dead man isn't really in the parade until the parade has reached the grave. The organists who once played between pitches understood the game's lithic agonies. Now, when the manager goes to the mound and calls for the relief pitcher the stadium fills with a hundred-decibel clip of the Beatles singing "Help!"

Ah me, the baseball moguls stole the still-beating heart from every ballpark when they took away the mighty Wurlitzers.

Once upon a time, those circus notes produced the stylized effect of largeness. The ancients called this "synaphea"—the overuse of a simple connective in a phrase:

"On this campaign went the Greeks and the Carians and the Lycians and the Pamphilians and the Phrygians."

Tromp. Tromp. Tromp.

Even though their numbers were small, how large they seemed, those armies!

The organ played while the manager walked to the mound and the crowd automatically felt the seriousness of the situation in its great, collective solar plexus.

I miss the organists.

Ballpark wisdom:

"This game is the only place where Americans face the fact that life is a matter of luck." *(Fan, male, middle-aged. The old Blue Jays Field in Toronto.)*

"The Red Sox get a man on first. Then they strand him there, all alone. And one guy ain't enough to leave alone." *(Male fan, a longtime sufferer. Fenway Park.)*

"When Derek Jeter is batting he's so awake—he's like Lady Macbeth!" *(Male fan, in his twenties, perhaps an English major, though not perfectly attentive. Yankee Stadium.)*

"Kiss me, ump! I'm beautiful!" *(Woman, fifty-something, her voice like gravel, laughing. Yankee Stadium.)*

Fenway Park. A male self-identified sociologist says, "The Boston fan likes the game more than the New York fan. Red Sox fans are contented with the ritual hunt for a victory. Yankee fans are only satisfied when they own the trophy."

"The Red Sox can't win because they have crickets in the outfield grass." *(A woman holding a baby in her arms.)*

"The Red Sox never win because a black cat walked across the infield back in 1978." *(Teenage boy who has studied his history.)*

"When Babe Ruth went to the New York Yankees he took Boston's ornaments of style. And baseball is a game of style." *(My own father. Fenway Park.)*

Closing Melodies:

Boston has defeated the Yankees, though their victory comes too late to save the season. A Boston College senior, a student of classical rhetoric, says wistfully, "We have robbed their bodies of steel, their coffers of silver, their fingers of gold."

28. *Alfred Whitehead Is Alive and Well in Corpus Christi, Texas*

"Listen," says Sam, "this is Corpus Christi. There's a sign on the wall behind you, 'All handguns must be licensed.' Half of these people are carrying a concealed weapon. But *listen* to them!"

I listen.

I hear diner noises: forks on plates, baritone laughter from a man who can't stop. Then a woman's laugh, snippy like scissors in a garden.

"They've all got guns and they're happy." Sam slaps the table, his wedding ring on the Formica.

"I mean, I come from Minnesota, I've been in Texas for three years. There's a cheerfulness here. People have broken hearts and they're cheerful. Their houses get flattened and they're cheerful. The spinster with the handbag has a gun in there and she's cheerful."

Sam is an Orientation and Mobility Specialist. He teaches blind people how to travel independently. He spends whole days with clients who are working their way back into the world. He knows about street crossings and the utility of listening. He's stirring sugar into an enormous glass of iced tea. He asks me if I've ever read the dialogues of Alfred North Whitehead.

"Some of them—things like 'why Edward VII wasn't a gentleman.'"

"Well he talks about how the rural people in America are indefatigably optimistic. The urban Americans have jobs with status and therefore they have something to lose. So people in the cities are pressured and pessimistic. But the rural American is flexible, upbeat, can make do with less. But Whitehead leaves out the guns."

"So you're saying there's a bonhomie that's discernible in the voices of gun-toters?"

"Yep! Just listen!"

"You're talking to a guy who thinks the opening minute of *The Magic Flute* sounds just like the Canadian national anthem. What am I listening for?"

"The trill, the exultation, the glory that comes with sitting on the big branch!"

I listen.

A throaty woman close by says, "Real cheese—I don't like that bogus shit!!"

Wild masculine laughter comes from the kitchen—a sound unrelated to the cheese woman.

A pay phone rings—with a genuine bell—a sound that's disappearing from America. No one answers it.

"Don't listen to the individual voices," says Sam. "Listen to the din . . . the general buzz . . ."

I crane my head. Fifty percent of the people in this diner are packing heat—imagining themselves as Bat Mastersons and Annie Oakleys.

"Sam, I can't hear it. I can't hear the *frisson!*" Jesus! I've used a French word in Texas!

"Turn your chair," Sam says.

"Do I get to ask questions while I'm listening?"

"Yes, ask questions. Whitehead approved of questions."

"Okay, according to Alfred Whitehead rural Americans were less concerned with losing it all than urban Americans—but did he say you could hear this in the tones of ordinary speech?"

"I don't know," Sam says.

"Did Whitehead listen to rural Americans?"

"I don't know that either."

"So in fact this is your idea—the Nyquist-Whitehead theory?"

"Rural Americans are more optimistic. That's Whitehead. And here in Corpus Christi everybody has a gun. And the locals are knee-slapping happy!"

He's right. It's July on the Gulf Coast of Texas and it's 114 degrees outside and here in this air-conditioned aluminum diner the ambient sound of the buzzing hive is festive.

I want to argue and so I suggest that the people of Moose Lake, Minnesota, when sitting in an air-conditioned Airstream diner on a brutally hot day, will sound in no way different than these pistol-packing Texans. So I say this and take a swig of iced tea.

"Ah! Moose Lake! Home of Elmer Fudd!" says Sam. "Have you ever been to Moose Lake?"

I admit that I visited Moose Lake once. It was a pilgrimage of sorts. I traveled fourteen hours on a Greyhound bus with a young poet from Finland. We were visiting Robert Bly, an American poet with a strong interest in Scandinavian literature.

"Okay, so did you go anywhere in public while you were there?"

"Well yes, in fact, we went to a diner."

"I know that diner. In reality it's a glorified closet."

"If I remember aright," I say, "it was built off the back of the owner's house."

"That's the place," says Sam. "Now tell me: what did you hear from the fair Minnesotans?"

I can tell he's enjoying himself. After three years in Texas Sam has become the self-styled Lévi-Strauss of low-fidelity diner noise. "Let's see. This was over twenty years ago. Reagan had just been elected. Carter was a lame duck. The whole country was in a dark frame of mind. I remember that when we went into the diner Robert Bly sized up the half dozen locals in the room and then pointed at Jarkko Laine, the Finnish poet, and said loudly, 'This is Jarkko! He's from Russia! He's here to buy your blue jeans!'"

"Great!" says Sam. "Did anyone react?"

"No. There was dead silence."

"Ah! Minnesota!" says Sam. "What else?"

"All right, let's see. This was a long time ago. I remember that there were three or four old guys wearing plaid hunting jackets who were sitting at a bar. I remember thinking that they must know Bly—the world-famous poet who just happens to live in their midst. I thought they probably think Bly is insane. The poet who talks to trees and rocks . . . So of course they didn't laugh. What else? We sat in a booth and drank coffee and talked about Russia, Finland, the Cold War, Reagan, Vietnam, poetry and politics, Neruda, the Swedish poet Tomas Tranströmer . . . We were rubbing sticks together trying to make a little fire in the Moose Lake Diner."

"You see? The locals in a Minnesota diner make almost no sound," says Sam, "they're like characters in a morality play—

the ones who just look left and right waiting for the figure of Death to appear."

"All right, but back to Whitehead for a minute. You can't get any more rural in America than Moose Lake. And those coffee drinkers were decidedly not members of the Optimists Club. I mean you hardly knew they were breathing."

"And you want to know," Sam interrupts, "how these moribund yokels square with the theory of rural optimism?"

"Sam, there wasn't one British thermal unit of optimism in Moose Lake."

"No guns," Sam says. "No guns, no diamonds, no music . . . here in Texas people are used to being poor. Texans make dough and lose it and expect to lose it. People here are just as poor as the rural northerners but they've got guns. All God's children got guns!"

I can't assail this principle. I think about it. Think about the photographs of Walker Evans, the people in Steinbeck, the traveling boys of the hobo jungles . . . did they have guns?

"No," says Sam. "Rural America arms herself in the seventies and eighties—now everyone carries a Glock, the woman pushing a stroller has more concealed firepower than John Wayne carried in *The Fighting Leathernecks*.

"So listen," he says.

It's true. The Texas diner is a temple of ebullience. Low-fidelity humming rises from all the throats—a liquid flow that pools on the ceiling. One man's tenor voice and another man's baritone are mixed with something mechanical, an industrial slicing machine—then the mezzo-soprano of a waitress skitters through the lake of sound like a rising seagull. The prevailing noise is like granules of charcoal in amplification. Crystals of life-force give off a static buzz when augmented electronically. This is the thing I hear: the happy electrolysis of people carrying weapons; a molecular symphony of potential violence. Everything is held together with the bonds of good eating. Guns rest under the diners' armpits or else they bulge on their waists. *In Texas*, say the molecules, *no one can take this laughter away* . . .

29. *In the Footsteps of Asklepios*

———◆———

My sister Carol is Asklepios, the doctor of Greek mysteries, the snake handler who stood just behind the caduceus. She was always the snake doctor, even as a girl. I have a memory of her at three or maybe four, dancing in New Hampshire under the pine trees. She had found a snake and was singing "La!" And the snake was writhing in a sunlit space at her feet. I remember how cheerful she sounded. I remember also that my mother was laughing, a thing she generally had trouble doing in the presence of children.

My sister was so delighted by that snake that she danced in a circle and imitated the snake's question marks with her hands. She danced on the hot sand. She threw her head back and laughed.

Twenty years later she studied choreography at Sarah Lawrence College in Bronxville, New York, and performed with dance companies around Brooklyn and Manhattan. She was the queen of serendipity, finding music by luck. She danced once to the Cuban drums on a discarded LP she'd found on a trash heap in Brooklyn. So for ten years she was a dancer to found objects in New York and now she's a medical doctor in that same city.

I was in college when I first became aware of the Greek doctor.

I was part of a group of students and we were touring Epidauros. We were tired from a badly delivered tourist board lecture about the Asklepios theater. We were walking the excavated pathways that circled through the sage bushes. The paths seemed to lead nowhere. The tour bus had broken down and it was a hot day. I sat under a tree. I remember that I wondered if "snake" was a verb before it was a noun. I was picturing Asklepios dancing the snake into the world of stones. I fell asleep then. My legs were splayed in the long sunlight and my head was in the night.

I remember that before I fell asleep and perhaps owing to the heat of the afternoon, I sensed that the whole world was silent. I had a peculiar feeling that everyone I knew was either dead or asleep. I woke to a sound of sheep bells. I knew then that Asklepios was genuine, like the green plums in the tree. Myth was like the clouds piling up. Asklepios, god of medicine, must have slept under a tree like this one and then he must have heard music and danced in broad and narrow circles as he remembered the dream. Asklepios: the surgeon, who owned a private grove of olive trees; who danced there with his snakes and his sheep.

My sister began medical school in her mid-thirties, horrified by the AIDS epidemic and having witnessed the deaths of numerous friends. She signed her matriculation papers and entered the subway on Lexington Avenue with a life-size acrylic human skeleton that swayed in her arms. The head was affixed to a metal stand. It was about five feet six inches tall. To make him sociable she placed a French beret on his skull. You can see anything in the subways. My sister Carol was moving in sympathy with the skeleton. The train hit a curve at 86th Street and she fell into the ribs and dipping legs. Then the train reversed its pitch and that skeleton was all over her like a sailor. A stranger, a man in a dark business suit, reached out and steadied the thing. "Does he get a name along with the beret?" he asked. Carol said he was André Malraux. "No one reads Malraux anymore," she said to me later. "I thought it was a good joke, *Man's Fate*."

Well how did Mr. Malraux get so clean? My sister's specimen was of course a synthetic creation. You can buy a genuine human skeleton for a higher price but the plastic version does the trick and is less expensive. How did Asklepios, who was once a real man, who was apotheosized into a god, how did he get his skeletons clean? It is believed that Asklepios used yellow snakes at Epidauros. They licked the bones of the dead. They cleaned the wounds of the sick. This is rumored to be the method. But it's certain that snakes won't perform without a dance. I'm not sure I'm prepared to say much more than that. One just understands that snake handlers and charmers are dancers. Such people dance without trouble or resistance.

Carol danced her skeleton down Fifth Avenue. His plastic bones clattered like the mechanism inside a player piano when the strings are muted.

I love the way my sister dances around the streets of New York City. I love following her and listening to the incidental sounds of her dancing.

One night my guide dog and I followed her down the street outside the Plaza Hotel. Carol was dressed entirely in red: red overcoat, red beret. She looked like one of the Manson girls— Squeaky Fromme. She had spotted a society lady dressed in mink. And so she fell in behind this woman, walking close, expertly shadowing the woman's back, imitating her every gesture with an easy, Chaplinesque manner. What I liked was the sound of her feet as she mimicked the grande dame. Carol smacked her feet flat against the pavement. Yellow leaves blew around the sidewalk. She was almost touching the back of the woman's mink stole. One can dance midway between a god and a devil. One can perform this dance anytime. The mink woman never suspected a thing.

I am not a dancer but I tried a little dance on that day in Epidauros. I whirled in circles on the excavated path of mysteries. I was in some sort of a half place. Two dead branches clicked somewhere behind me. Sometimes the branches sounded like children tapping. The crickets were perfectly loud and insensate in the midday heat. My feet slapped on the stones. I wondered if I could make a sound out of my own nature. Such dancing is injunctive—you jump into the world because moving is the only claim you need to make. I heard movement in the tall grass. My sandals on the worn stones sounded like blocks of wood clapping together.

When my sister decided to become a doctor she thought she would have to put aside her dancing. But during those years of exhaustive study I noticed that when we walked around New York her feet were inexorably drawn to rhythmic expression. One snowy night she danced carelessly around the Washington Square Arch. It was one of those moments when the entire city seems asleep. The new snow was coming hard and the only sound in the street was the occasional taxi spinning its wheels. Carol danced around the monument to the echoes of her own voice as it bounced off the great arch. She was dancing to laughter. The human voice has a bright roundness in these moments. Earlier that week she had performed an autopsy on her first human cadaver. She'd opened the casket to find a cyanotic blue woman who looked, despite her color, like someone's grandmother. When you operate on a cadaver you're not supposed to know the identity of the corpse. But a mistake had been made:

there was a toe tag with the woman's name written in block letters. And my sister talked to her and talked and danced in large and small circles according to what had to be done. In Greek dance, the place, the physical plot of earth, gives its voice to the one who dances. My sister removed the old woman's brain in that spirit.

After I danced alone in Epidauros I rejoined the bus tour. Around sunset we stopped in a fishing village. A group of college kids decided to swim from a stone embankment and so they jumped into the sea and I joined them and the water was bitterly cold. We swam in tight circles for about ten minutes. Then we headed for the quay. The boy in the lead pressed his feet on a submerged stone and reached up the rock wall with his hands. He let out a shriek. The sunken stones were covered with spiny sea urchins. He clambered over rocks and there were spines in his feet and hands. Some of the swimmers began to panic and threw themselves at the stones in a rush. They were stung repeatedly. Boys and girls were weeping as they reached the top. I was the last one in the sea. I was preparing myself for the stingers. I knew they would feel like hornet stings. I thought about my dance along the path in Epidauros. I'd heard the rustling of snakes. I didn't know if my dancing had scared them or attracted them. But I thought of them as I reached for the stones. And I pulled myself up the seawall without receiving a single sting.

My sister completed her residency while working in some of New York's most impoverished charity hospitals. I heard her say one night: "All ecstatic propositions are extreme, including health." The Greek snake doctor would agree. Listen for the small tongues. The sound of a cure is like the songs of the earth. One night in the ER my sister heard the sound of maggots falling from a homeless woman's pants. *Das Lied von der Erde.*

Listening in the city is an acquired skill. My sister, who would dance strangers into health if she only could, taught me how to hear on the streets of New York.

Once the snakes have opened your ears you notice all kinds of things.

I've heard the hooves of police horses when the cops must clear the subway tracks of drunks.

I've heard a Russian man talk to his horse about God.

I've heard the snubbed noses of stopped cars snorting.

I've pictured the faces behind those windshields, faces wrinkled and hearing only the pull of time.

Sometimes I've heard a horn far back in the mass of stopped cars, a horn from someone who still remembers yearning for wind. I know he's a sailor. He's reconstructing the ocean in his mind. His only instrument at that moment is the automobile. And the only sea at that moment is the street in New York.

I've heard how the wind pushes the smallest birds.

I think of the birds in New York as bits of burning glass . . .

I make it through the curtain of threatening sound.

I make it because listening like Asklepios one is both dark and clear.

The old Greek doctor is all ears, teeth, and heart.

The followers of Asklepios rolled carved wooden balls through the grass to rouse the snakes. They knew that men would get better if they learned to hear the small things all around them.

Epilogue

◆

It's easy to listen in childhood when all the songs are new. The first birds demand nothing from us.

Later we find that sounds can call us to grow.

I went to Tallinn when the Russians were still occupying that beautiful place. I was twenty-seven but immature for my age. I'd gone to Estonia for a dishonorable purpose: I was on a drunkard's tour. In those days people from Helsinki—men mostly—would ride the Soviet ferries across the Baltic and spend the weekend drinking cheap vodka in hotels that had been erected just for them. I was curious. I wanted to witness "fear and loathing in Tallinn."

I remember the following sounds:

Four hundred smashed Finns swarmed through the Soviet passport control. I was in the back of the throng because I was an American and would have to go through a special inspection. I had to wait. I can attest that the noise of four hundred drunken men pushing and cursing their way through a gate is unlike the sound of a Hollywood stampede. Their boots made the noise of dried blood. Those boots made the metaphysical noise called "the edge of night"—there really is no other way to describe it.

When it was my turn to enter, the Soviet guard looked me up and down, then examined my papers. He pressed a button and a buzzer buzzed and another officer appeared—a woman who spoke English.

"Why do you not look like you?" she asked.

"Is that a metaphysical question?" I asked.

"You have a passport and a visa," she said, "and neither photograph looks like you."

"Sometimes I am depressed and sometimes I'm happy," I said. Then, because I was immature, I performed a little dance with windmill gestures and many facial expressions.

"I see," said the Russian woman. "You are stupid."

"Yes," I said, "I am stupid."

I was feeling a tapering faintness around my ears.

The woman did something with a ring of keys. This was not going well.

"Come this way," she said.

"I am blind," I said, "you will have to assist me."

"You are blind?" She paused.

I heard the straggling drunks laughing off in the distance. One of them had dropped a bottle. Apparently the bottle hadn't broken. "Oh my baby, my baby," a man said.

"Here, I will adopt your baby," another man said.

"No, no," said the first man, "you will not give my baby the right education." They laughed that roving laugh of big men, a laugh I've never been able to master. That's what I was thinking as the woman from the Red Army was reexamining me.

"You are blind and you have come here by yourself?" she said after a moment.

"Yes, I've come to Tallinn to hear music," I said.

"We will have to search you," she said.

I was wishing that I could speak Russian. I wanted to say

that I was nauseated and pleased at the same time. Almost certainly there would be a Russian word for this. Evidently the Soviet Union thought I was such a good listener that I would have to be searched.

"Come with me," she said. She grabbed my arm. She took me to a small room.

"You are to take off your clothes," she said.

It occurred to me that if they had my clothing they could plant listening devices somewhere and then accuse me of being a spy. Why had I said I'd come to hear music? How foolish! Why hadn't I said I was here to get drunk?

As I began taking off my shirt the woman talked steadily to a man who had appeared without a sound.

They spoke back and forth like two severed wings.

My hands were shaking and I was having trouble with my buttons.

They were looking through my bag.

Suddenly the man said in English: "Don't bother with your clothes. Have a nice time in the Soviet Union."

Had he put a listening device in my bag? Had he decided that I was merely brainless?

I was suitably frightened and headed directly to the hotel, where I stayed and drank vodka for the next twelve hours. I knew some students in that dedicated collection of drinkers. I talked openly about my fear that the Russians wouldn't let me out of the country. As I downed vodka and nattered away I convinced myself that I would be arrested as soon as I tried to depart.

The next day I followed a student group from Finland as they walked the old town in the center of Tallinn. I was badly hungover. Sand shifted and spread out inside me. My body blundered ahead. The cobblestones made walking very hard.

Around this time our little group decided to attend church. *Oh God*, I thought, *I'm too ill to attend church.*

But I went along. I knew I was unable to get back to the hotel without assistance. And I thought of how pleasant it would be to sit. There would be music. Yes. And if the border guards asked me what I'd done in Estonia I could say I'd been listening to music.

To this day I can't describe the church. Upon entering I was separated from my group and therefore I had no one to paint a word picture for me. I sat alone among the indistinct many. I had no idea what house of worship we had entered.

Then the organ poured out its red and black sound—the pipe organ that has always made me think about milk and iodine—that huffed-up and scared instrument. Its very mechanism floods the fields and freezes them in the same instant—that organ was now over us.

The hidden organist was playing Bach.

It was the "Little" Prelude and Fugue in E minor. Or I thought it was. The notes began to move from one side of my brain to the other as they were meant to. And how green and sick I was feeling. And Bach, who wrote on the far side of midnight, and this organist, who was also on the far side—they were expanding the circle of light, the "nimbus," if you will, of Christian humility. This was how Bach was going to find me just there in that dark church. Numbers and midnight and fear in a young life . . . A boy's life really . . . What did he know anyway? The silken shape of Bach's hat fell onto him, as it always does for all who will listen.

A priest began to speak. He was reciting in Latin. We had come to the old Estonian Catholic Church of St. Peter and St. Paul. The priest's voice had a prying quality but it was warm: the man had tenderness about him.

Without warning a woman cried out. "Jesu!" Her voice had a kernel of darkness—her voice took on weight as it rose. It was a twining, gathering call. Other women were crying then. The church was very dim. I could see only the blackness or greens of a forest and thin openings of light that must have been from candles. "Jesu, Jesu," came the call.

It was the first time I'd ever heard communitarian weeping: it was a dedicated, pilgrimming song.

It didn't have a single Puritan note. It came from too far back.

Someone, perhaps it was the priest, rang a small bell.

A bell defines you when you're not expecting it. The sound of a bell marks your life. It says you will make your part of the road whether you will it or you don't. The priest rang the bell again. It gave up a sound of curiosity and of early summer.

The bell was in the key of A. At least I thought it was.

That bell said we should walk in the warming fields.

Then I was back in the streets of Tallinn. I was alone and walking a narrow lane. I heard bells from six churches, each sounding its beckoning refrain from a corner of the city. I knew I could travel solely for the music and the music would always be unpredictable and it would never fade away.

ACKNOWLEDGMENTS

Grateful acknowledgment is made to the editors of publications in which sections of this book (some in earlier versions) first appeared: *Backwards City, Riverteeth, The Fourth Genre,* and *The Bark.* A brief section of chapter ten appeared earlier in a different form in an essay entitled "Fatland," which is included in the nonfiction anthology *Scoot Over, Skinny,* published by Harcourt and edited by Donna Jarrell and Ira Sukrungruang.

The epigraph from Susan Ludvigson's "What If" is used with her permission. The poem was published in the collection *Sweet Confluences* (Louisana University Press, 2000.)

I wish to thank the MacDowell Colony, of Peterborough, New Hampshire, for a residency which allowed me to complete some of the sections in this book.

Thanks also to Sharon Bryan, Eric Gnezda, Judith Kitchen, Susan Ludvigson, Lia Purpura, David Reilly, Stan Rubin, Andrea Sarpino, Peggy Shumaker, Deborah Tall, Ken Weisner, David Weiss, and Gary Whittington for their good counsel and friendship during the writing of this book. Thanks also to Bill and Norma Rudloff—the finest in-laws in the world.

I also owe thanks to my colleagues at Ohio State: Brenda

Brueggemann, Valerie Lee, Brian McHale, Richard Green, Les Tannenbaum, Scott Lissner, and Debra Moddelmog.

I owe special gratitude to Clete and Anne Baier of Bow, New Hampshire. Summer is always with them.

Additional thanks are offered here to the staff of Fay's Boat Yard, and in particular Steve, Bernie, and Merrill—all of these good men have kept my family afloat.

I wish to acknowledge two departed friends and colleagues: Ted Zubrycki and David See. Both were excellent guide-dog trainers and lifelong supporters of the blind. All who knew them will never forget their works and days.

ABOUT THE AUTHOR

STEPHEN KUUSISTO is a graduate of the Writers' Workshop at the University of Iowa and was a Fulbright Scholar. He teaches at The Ohio State University in Columbus, where he specializes in disability studies. He is the author of *Planet of the Blind: A Memoir,* a *New York Times* Notable Book of the Year for 1998, and *Only Bread, Only Light,* a collection of poems. He is coeditor (with Deborah Tall and David Weiss) of *The Poet's Notebook: Excerpts from the Notebooks of Contemporary American Poets.*

Visit Steve at www.stephenkuusisto.com.

CPSIA information can be obtained at www.ICGtesting.com
Printed in the USA
LVOW06s1900260314

379049LV00009B/1306/P